# HAVERHILL, MASSACHUSETTS
# TRIVIA BOOK

## Trivia Questions and Activities
## for Fun and Learning

*including*

### Biographies of Haverhill Citizen's
### Hall of Fame Inductees

*E. Philip Brown and Pat Garwich*

*Haverhill Public Schools*

iUniverse, Inc.
Bloomington

**HAVERHILL, MASSACHUSETTS**
**TRIVIA QUESTIONS AND ACTIVITIES FOR FUN AND LEARNING**

*iUniverse books may be ordered through booksellers or by contacting:*

*iUniverse*
*1663 Liberty Drive*
*Bloomington, IN 47403*
*www.iuniverse.com*
*1-800-Authors (1-800-288-4677)*

*ISBN: 978-1-4759-8955-7 (sc)*
*ISBN: 978-1-4759-8953-3 (e)*

*Library of Congress Control Number: 2013908154*

*Printed in the United States of America.*

*iUniverse rev. date: 5/2/2013*

## Rationale

There is a need, in my opinion, for children to learn the history, geography and contributions of the citizens of the city in which they live. We are all aware of our own neighborhoods, shopping areas and places of personal relevance. All too frequently we pass monuments, buildings and historical markers without notice. We all stand on the shoulders of dead men. By that, I mean That we are at our present level of progress because of the contributions of all who have proceeded us. Perhaps this thought will help us to understand the necessity of planning for the future.

Our city is rich in history, diverse cultures and multiple resources - written, physical, and human - eager to share knowledge, experience, memories and artifacts. It is fervently hoped that this booklet of trivia questions will spark an interest in pursuing more information on our city, assist others in tapping our resources, instill a sense of pride in our community and maybe even inspire some of our young people to match and surpass the achievements of past Haverhillites.

## Objectives

- to teach about our city in an informative manner – tapping a method that students enjoy - trivia questions.
- to instill pride in our community.
- to encourage research and utilization of reference materials as well as human resources.
- to foster the discovery that many Haverhillites have attained fame and fortune through perserverence.
- to raise -the consciousness level regarding the fact that actions of citizens today affect the citizens of tomorrow.
- to pique the curiosity of students regarding their personal heritage.
- to create an awareness of the physical, cultural, and historical environment in which we live.
- to be utilized as daily challenges, time fillers, "Jeopardy" questions and Academic Bowl questions as well as research topics.

*- Patricia Garwich*

# Haverhill, Massachusetts TRIVIA BOOK

## Table Of Contents

# 1873 Description of Haverhill

Haverhill is an enterprising and uncommonly beautiful city, noted for the manufacture of boots and shoes, and for its recent growth and industrial prosperity. It lies in the northerly part of Essex County, on the left bank of the Merrimack River, at the head of the tide-water and of sloop-navigation.

It contains three postal centres, - Haverhill, East Haverhill, and Ayer's Village, - 280 farms, 1,975 dwelling-houses, and 12,092 inhabitants, with a valuation of $10,234,90, and a tax-rate of $1.74 PER $100. The Indian name of this place was Pentucket.

The surface of the city is agreeably diversified with rounded hills, valleys, lakes, stream, and river; and the populous part of the city, occupying a gentle acclivity rising immediately from the brink of the Merrimack, presents, with its handsome private residences, its churches, and other public edifices, a remarkably fine appearance.

There are some excellent farms and apple-orchards here, and considerable attention is given to market-gardening; but the principal business is manufacturing . The city has establishments for making woollen-goods, hats, shoe-lasts, shoe nails and tacks, boxes, tin-ware, and clothing; and about 150 firms are busily employed in the making of boots and shoes.

The city proper has many handsome streets, lined with commodious stores, manufactories, public and private buildings, which are well supplied with water from the lake above

The settlement at Haverhill was commenced in 1640 by the Rev. John Ward and others, who accompanied him from Newbury. The land was purchased of the Indians Passaquo and Saggahew Nov. 15, 1642, and then extended 14 miles upon the river, and from it six miles north, embracing parts of Methuen, and of Salem, Atkinson, and Plaistow in New Hampshire. It was named in memory of Haverhill, the birthplace of Mr. Ward in England, and incorporated in 1645. The plantation then contained about 32 landholders, and was, with the exception of open fields upon the river, a dense and unbroken forest. In 1650 it was voted "that Abraham Tyler blow his horn half an hour before meeting on the Lord's day and on lecture-days, and receive one pound of pork annually for his services from each family." A bell was not procured until 1748.

*- An excerpt from Gazetteer of Massachusetts written by the Rev. Elias Nason, M.A. in 1873*

## Geography Trivia

Q: How big is Haverhill?
A: Roughly nine miles long by five and a half miles wide, 21,955.5 acres.

Q: What is the length of the tidal shore line of Haverhill?
A: 16.8 miles

Q: What county is Haverhill in?
A: Essex County

Q: Name the seven bodies of water in Haverhill.
A: Kenoza Lake, Crystal Lake, Millvale Reservoir, Lake Saltonstall also known as Plugged Pond, Lake Pentucket also known as Round Pond. Chadwick's Pond, Frye's Pond.

Q: How far is Haverhill from our state's capitol?
A: Approximately 33 miles.

Q: How many counties are in Massachusetts?
A: Fourteen

Q: Haverhill is located in which corner of the state?
A: Northeast

Q: What state borders Haverhill to the north?
A: New Hampshire

Q: Which ocean is east of Haverhill?
A: The Atlantic Ocean

Q: The mouth of the Merrimack River empties into which ocean?
A: The Atlantic Ocean

Q: What town borders Haverhill to the northeast?
A: Merrimac

Q: Which two towns border Haverhill on the south?
A: Groveland and Boxford

Q: What town borders Haverhill to the east?
A: West Newbury

## Demographics Trivia

Q: What is the population of Haverhill?
A: 62,373 per 2010 Census

Q: Are there more males or more females in Haverhill
A: 2010 Census; 32,442 females - 29,931 males

Q: How many people per square mile?
A: 1,871.5 as of March 2012

Q: How many churches are there in Haverhill?
A: Forty

Q: Where does Haverhill rank in the state in terms of population?
A: Fifteenth

Q: What is the median age in Haverhill?
A: 35.2

Q: What are the percentages of Haverhill's population by race?
A: White: 82.31%
   Black or African American – 3.25%
   American Indian and Alaska Native – .09%
   Asian – 1.83%
   Native Hawaiian and other
        Pacific Islander – .1%
   Other – 12.52%

Q: What are the percentages of Haverhill's population by ethnicity?
A: Hispanic: 12.8%
   Non-Hispanic: 87.20

## Government Trivia

Q: What type of government does Haverhill have?
A: Mayor - Council

Q: Who is the Mayor of Haverhill?
A: James J. Fiorentini

Q: How many members are on the city council?
A: Nine.

Q: Who are current members of the city council?
A: Council President Robert H. Scatamacchia
Council Vice President Michael J. Hart
Councillor John A. Michitson
Councillor William H. Ryan
Councillor Michael S. McGonagle
Councillor William J. Macek
Councillor Colin F. LePage
Councillor Mary Ellen Daly O'Brien
Councillor Thomas Sullivan

Q: Who is the Chief of Police?
A: Chief Alan R. DeNaro

Q: Who is the fire chief?
A: Chief Richard Borden

Q: Who is the director of the Haverhill Public Library?
A: Carol Verny

Q: Who is the City Clerk?
A: Margaret Toomey

Q: Who is the Economic Development Director?
A: William Pillsbury

Q: Who is the Human Services Director?
A: Vincent Oullette

Q: Who represents Haverhill in Congress?
A: Sen. Elizabeth R. Warren, Sen. Mo Cowan (temporary), Rep. Niki Tsongas

Q: Who represents Haverhill at the State House?
A: Sen. Kathleen O'Connor Ives, Rep. Linda Dean Campbell Rep. Brian Dempsey, Diana DiZoglio, Rep. Jim Lyons, Rep. Leonard Mirra

## Education Trivia

Q: What is the motto of Haverhill Public Schools?
A: "Live and Let Live"

Q: Who is the superintendent of schools?
A: James F. Scully

Q: How many members are on the School Committee?
A: Seven:
Mayor James Fiorentini
Susan Danehy – President
Paul A. Magliochetti – Vice-President
Shaun Toohey
Joseph Bevilacqua
Raymond Sierpina
Scott Wood Jr.

Q: The statue in front of Haverhill High School is commonly called "The Thinker". What is its correct name?
A: Il Pensieroso

Q: Who sculpted the original statue?
A: Michaelangelo

Q: In 1803 Bradford Academy opened. It was the second oldest school in the country for the higher education of women. What is it known as today?
A: Zion Bible College

Q: What is the oldest middle school in Haverhill?
A: John Greenleaf Whittier (1958)

Q: What is the most recently built middle school in Haverhill?
A: Dr. A.B. Consentino School (1969)

Q: What elementary school was once called the "Brain Factory"?
A: Tilton School (1891)

Q: Which school is the largest elementary school in the city?
A: Bradford Elementary School

Q: Which is the largest middle school in the city?
A: Dr. A.B Consentino School

Q: What is the name of the Whittier School athletic teams?
A: "Poets"

Q: What is the name of the Consentino School athletic teams?
A: "Chargers"

Q: What is the name of the Nettle School athletic teams?
A: "Knights"

Q: What is the name of the Hunking School athletic teams?
A: "Bobcats"

Q: What is the name of the Haverhill High School athletic teams?
A: "Hillies"

Q: What is a Hillie?
A: A minuteman who mans a cannon on a hilltop.

Q: What is the name of the Whittier Regional Vocational Technical High School athletic teams?
A: "Wildcats"

Q: What is the name of the school in Bradford that was once the Bradford Academy?
A: Greenleaf

Q: What is the name of the oldest school in the city that is still being used as a school?
A: Greenleaf School

Q: What year did Northern Essex Community College begin operations in Haverhill?
A: 1961

Q: When was Haverhill High School on Monument Street opened?
A: 1963

Q: In what year did Bradford College become a coeducational school?
A: 1971

Q: What year did Haverhill Trade School start?
A: 1924

Q: Who was a Haverhill teacher who authored several arithmetic books? A school has been named in his honor.
A: Benjamin Greenleaf

Q:What was the name of the St. James School sport's teams?
A: the Saints

Q: Which school was built on the site of the old Lithuanian Grove?
A: Bradford Elementary School

Q: Who is superintendent of Whittier Regional Technical School?
A: William DeRosa

## Sports Trivia

Q: Who set the Girl's Swimming MIAA All-State meet record in the 50-yard freestyle with a time of 23.62 on Nov. 22, 1998. That record still stands.
A: Paige Crimmin

Q: Which former Hillie was American League Comeback Player of the Year and was considered as an AL MVP candidate in 2007. He also was named the Player's Choice AL Comeback Player of the Year by fellow players.
A: Carlos Pena

Q: Who was the Haverhill resident who won a gold medal in the 1964 Olympics?
A: Gerry Ashworth, 400 meter relay team- in Austria.

Q: What Haverhill man was a golf pro who gave lessons to President Eisenhower?
A: George Astor (1908-1981)

Q: Which Haverhill native was the first girl admitted into the Little League in the United States?
A: Sharon Poole in 1972

Q: Which Haverhill native umpired in the National League from 1968 to his untimely death in 1987. He wore uniform number 18 for most of his career. He umpired in two World Series, two All-Star Games and five League Championship Series?
A: Dick Stello

Q: Who was the famous exotic dancer and actress that was married Dick Stello?
A: Chesty Morgan

Q: Which Haverhill native was a catcher for the Boston Red Sox on the 1967 "Impossible Dream Team"?
A: Mike Ryan

Q: Which Haverhill High football player played in the 1934 Rose Bowl for Columbia University?
A: Joe Rich

Q: Which HHS and Boston College football star was elected to the National Football Foundation's College Football Hall of Fame in 1982?
A: Eugene Goodreault

Q: What two recent years did the Haverhill High School Girls Basketball team win state championships?
A: 1995 and 1996

Q: Which professional baseball player from Haverhill helped the Red Sox win the 1915 and 1916 World Series?
A: Harold Chandler "Hal" Janvrin

Q: Which former Haverhill teacher held the most track, field, and running championships in New England at the time of his death in 1987?
A: Anthony Sapienza

Q: Who held three national boxing championships including the Jr. Welterweight Championship under the guidance and training of Mr. Mickey Ward. He was also widely known for his two season appearances on NBC's hit reality TV show "The Contender" in 2005 and 2006?
A: Jeff Fraza

Q: Who was named to the United States Ski Team in 1965, and after graduating college, was a top ranking amateur in the East? He continued his ski racing career for many years and was a National Masters Champion.
A: Roger Buchika

Q: Which Hillie running back played for Boston College and was drafted by the Buffalo Bills?
A: Dan Conway, Class of '76

Q: When was the Haverhill Stadium wall built?
A: 1937 (W.P.A. project)

Q: What was the name of Haverhill Stadium changed to in 2011?
A: Trinity EMS Stadium

Q: Who is the Trinity EMS Stadium field dedicated to?
A: Harry McNamara 1936-2010

Q: Who is the Haverhill High School pool named after?
A: Charles C. White

Q: When was the Veterans Memorial Skating Rink built?
A: 1972

Q: What is the Haverhill High fight song?
A: "Stand Up and Cheer"

Q: What are the lyrics to "Stand and Cheer"?
A: Stand Up and Cheer
We're going to win for dear o'le Haverhill
For today...we'll raise the flag
above the blue, above the blue

Our team is fighting
and we are bound to win or die.

We're going to win..rah...rah
We're going to win..rah...rah

We're going to win for Haverhill High!!!

*Lyrics provided by Jane Comeau, Class of 1974*

Q: What year did the Haverhill Baseball Team win the New England Pennant?
A: 1904

Q: How many golf courses are there in Haverhill?
A: Six.
Bradford Country Club
Crystal Lake Golf Course
Garrison Golf Center
Haverhill Golf & Country Club
Renaissance Golf Club
Northfields

Q: What popular Haverhill jeweler pitched his way to the top of the Red Sox farm system?
A: Irving "Sheik" Karelis

Q: What Haverhill resident was signed up a as a goalie for the New England Revolution in 2010?
A: Tim Murray

## Arts, Entertainment, and Literature Trivia

Q: Who painted the murals in City Hall? At that time it was Haverhill High School.
A: Prescott Baston in 1930.

Q: Where is the Quaker poet, John Greenleaf Whittier, buried?
A: Union Cemetery, Amesbury, MA

Q: What Haverhill native, artist and author, painted a miniature of a dog for the Duchess of Windsor?
A: Gladys Emerson Cook

Q: What Haverhill resident was a cartoonist and creator of "Archie" comics based on Haverhill High School experiences?
A: Bob Montana (1920-1975)

Q: What Haverhill resident became a star of the Metropolitan Opera?
A: Cora Chase (Williamson)(1892-1984)

Q: Name the Haverhill artist whose painting of a sailing vessel entitled "The Alert" was used in Richard Dana's book, Two Years Before the Mast.
A: Sidney Chase ( L877-1957)

Q: Name the Haverhill woman whose poem "Love of Life" was displayed at the 1939 World's Fair.
A: Frances Cole Lee

Q: Who was the Haverhill born television and movie actress, mother-in-law of Cloris Leachman and sister of Jack Albertson?
A: Madeline Albertson, T.V. series "Those Whiting Girls". Movie "Home before Dark"

Q: Who first translated the stories of "Cinderella" and "Sleeping Beauty" into English and owned a printing shop on Water Street in 1794 ?
A: Publisher Peter Edes, translated "Perreault's Fairy Tales"

Q: Who was Haverhill's most famous resident, poet, and abolitionist?
A: John Greenleaf Whittier (1807 - 1881)

Q: The 2004 movie *We Don't Live Here Anymore* is based on two novellas by which former Bradford College professor?
A: Andre Dubus

Q: Who was the Russian born immigrant who started a theatrical business in Haverhill and became head of MGM Studios in Hollywood, California?
A: Louis B. Mayer

Q: Which graduate of the HHS Class of 1976 wrote the novel House of Sand and Fog (1999) which was a finalist for the National Book Award and the basis for an Academy award-nominated film.
A: Andre Dubus III

Q: Who is the Haverhill born composer who wrote "Manhattan Serenade"?
A: Louis Alter

Q: Which book by Andre Dubus III was on the New York Times best-seller list for six weeks, rising as high as number four.
A: Townie

Q: Who was the Haverhill born and author horticulturalist and author who had his own television show on gardening?
A: James U. Crockett (1915-1979)

Q: Who became Miss USA in 1967?
A: Sylvia Hitchcock Carson

Q: Name the Haverhill author who served as a member of Franklin Delano Roosevelt's "Brain Trust".
A: Stuart Chase (1888-1985)

Q: Who was the Haverhill born comedian who appeared on television with Jackie Gleason?
A: Frank Fontaine (1920-1978)

Q: Who was the Haverhill born singer called "The Irish Queen"?
A: Maggie Cline Ryan (1857-1934)

Q: Which Haverhill High graduate won his first of two Emmy Awards in 2000 for being host of Hollywood Squares.
A: Tom Bergeron

Q: What famous artist was born in Haverhill and died in Egypt?
A: Henry Bacon (1839-1912)

Q: Name a famous Haverhill resident who is the author of children's books.
A: John Bellairs

Q: Which Haverhill High School graduate shock-rocker has sold over 15 million albums worldwide, and has had six Top 20 hits on the Billboard Hot Mainstream Rock Tracks chart in the United States?
A: Robb Zombie born Robert Bartleh Cummings

Q: What is the title of John Greenleaf Whittier's most famous poem?
A: "Snowbound"

Q: What is the title of the Essex Street Gateway Mural?
A: "Hues of the Heart"

Q: The title of the 2003 movie 21 Grams refers to a theory about the weight of the human soul proposed by which Haverhill doctor.
A: Dr. Duncan MacDougall.

Q: What was the name of WHAV's most popular call-in show?
A: Bill Pike on the Open Mike

Q: What Haverhill native played Nick Barkley on *The Big Valley*?
A: Peter Breck

Q: Haverhill was referred to, but mispronounced, in the 2006 series finale of which popular NBC TV show.
A: West Wing

Q: Which dancer for Haverhill has danced alongside Neil Patrick Harris in the opening number of "The 82nd Annual Academy Awards" and has been on "Dancing With The Stars"?
A: Channing Cooke

Q: Which Haverhill baker was on the Food Network's Food Network Challenge in 2001 and has provided baked goods for late-night show host Conan O'Brien, car sales mogul Ernie Boch Jr., the Make-A-Wish Foundation, and the cast of "Jesus Christ Superstar."
A: Erin Erler of Cakes by Erin

Q: What is the name of Howard Sterns' first wife who was from Haverhill?
A: Alison Berns

Q:  Who is the Bradford college professor and historians who has written several books on Haverhill's history such as *A New England City, Haverhill, Massachusetts, Irish in Haverhill, Italians in Haverhil, and Haverhill, Massachusetts: From Town To City.*
A: Patricia Trainor O'Malley Ph.D.

Q: Popular only in the Merrimack Valley, which card game was brought to Haverhill by Irish  immigrants?
A: Forty-fives

Q: Which Haverhill Trade School graduate and entertainer was the first person to develop the use of live music played over recorded tracks?
A: Billy Fellows

Q: Who was known as the "bareback horse rider and circus queen"?
A: Helen Gertrude Wilson Bartlett or Gert Swasey

Q: Which heavy metal band recorded their second album in Haverhill?
A: Godsmack

Q: Who is the Las Vegas entertainer and actor who got his start in a McDonald's commercial?
A: Brian Evans

Q: Which author modeled a college that was in several of his books after Bradford College ?
A: H.P. Lovecraft

Q: Which Haverhill native was named New England Country Music Organization's Female vocalist and entertainer of the year in 2012? ?
A: Jillian Cardarelli

# General Knowledge of Haverhill Trivia

Q: How many radio stations in Haverhill?
A: Two WXRV 92.5 FM – " The River" and WHAV 1640 AM (covers northern Haverhill only)

Q: What is a weir?
A: A fish trap. They were once used in Little River.

Q: Name five presidents that have been in Haverhill?
A: George Washington, John Quincy Adams, Harry S. Truman, William H Taft & Theodore Roosevelt.

Q: What is the most famous landmark in Haverhill?
A: John Greenleaf Whittier's Birthplace.

Q: When was Whittier's Birthplace built?
A: 1688

Q: What is the oldest street in Haverhill?
A: Mill Street

Q: What is the oldest street in Bradford?
A: Ferry Street

Q: What town was originally part of Bradford?
A: Groveland

Q: What is a "gundalow"?
A: A flat bottomed barge that was used for transporting hay and goods along the Merrimack River.

Q: When did radio station WHAV go into operation?
A: 1947

Q: Who was the first mayor of Haverhill?
A: Warner R. Whittier in 1870

Q: Who is the longest serving mayor in Haverhill history?
A: Mayor James J. Fiorentini

Q: Where in Haverhill can one see a button from the coat of George Washington?
A: Haverhill Historical Society - "Buttonwoods"

Q: "Buttonwoods" is the name given to the Haverhill Historical Society and a museum on Water Street. The trees were called "buttonwoods". What kind of tree are they?
A: Sycamore

Q: How many gallons of water are used daily in Haverhill
A: Avg daily production 2011:
   4 million gallons
 Peak production day 2011:
   8.7 million gallons
 Avg use/person/day 2011: 64 gallons
 Annual production 2011: 1,966,878,370 gallons

Q: How many miles of road does the City of Haverhill maintain?
A: 230 miles Note: This does not include state roads

Q: What was the original water supply for the first Haverhill settlers?
A: Plugged Pond

Q: Which endangered species of fish spawns in the Merrimack River in Haverhill?
A: Shortnose Sturgeon

Q: The reverse of the swastika was a symbol used by the Indians. What did it mean?
A: Good luck

Q: Winnekenni is an Indian word. What does it mean?
A: Very Beautiful

Q: Great Pond is known today by the name John Greenleaf Whittier gave it. What is the name?
A. Kenoza Lake

Q: Kenoza is an Indian word. What does it mean?
A: Pickerel

Q: What is the name of the oldest cemetery in Haverhill?
A: Pentucket Cemetery (corner of Water and Mill Streets)

Q: Four naval destroyers in WWI were named for Haverhill men. Name them
A: Moody, Sharkey, Perkins, Crowell

Q Which United States president received a part of his education in Haverhill?
A: John Quincy Adams

Q: What was the name of Haverhill's first newspaper started in 1793?
A: The Guardian of Freedom

Q: When did The Haverhill Gazette start operations?
A: 1821

Q: What is the name of the first newspaper in the world to receive news by telephone?
A: The Haverhill Gazette

Q: Our city was first known as Pentucket. How did it get the name Haverhill?
A: The first preacher was John Ward. He was highly respected and came from Haverhill, England. Our city was named in his honor, for his home town.

Q: Pentucket was an Indian name. What does it mean?
A: Place of the winding river.

Q: What is the oldest wooden frame house in Haverhill?
A: The John Ward House.

Q: What famous landmark was built in 1874 entirely of stones found in the area?
A: Winnekenni Castle.

Q: What was the Haverhill made product that won a bronze medal at the Chicago Exposition in 1893?
A: A shoe. (It can be found at Buttonwoods)

Q: What Haverhill house is built of bricks and was brought here from England as ballast on ships?
A: Peaslee Garrison House on East Broadway, Rocks Village.

Q: How many beds are in the Merrimack Valley Hospital?
A: MVH is licensed for 108 beds

Q: How many names on the Civil War Monument in Monument Square at the junction of Main and Kenoza Avenue?
A: 187

Q: Which Haverhill cemetery has the graves of 415 Civil War soldiers and veterans?
A: Hilldale Cemetery

Q: Where is the Spanish War Memorial?
A: Gale Park on Kenoza Avenue

Q: How many names are there on the Spanish War Memorial?
A: 313

Q: What is the Spanish War Memorial statue called?
A: "The Hiker"

Q: Haverhill was the first community east of the Mississippi to adopt the commission form of government. When did this happen? What is it?
A: 1908. Mayor-four aldermen

Q: When was Haverhill incorporated as a town?
A: 1645

Q: John D. Osgood invented what common heating system device in Haverhill?
A: The thermostat

Q: What does G.A.R. Park mean?
A: Grand Army of the Republic

Q: What year was the "Great Fire" that destroyed most of Washington Street and much of the shoe industry?
A: 1882

Q: When did the Haverhill Chamber of Commerce begin?
A: 1888

Q: Where in Haverhill is there a "cobbler" shop with all of the tools and materials to make shoes?
A: Buttonwoods Museum.

Q: Who started the Haverhill Boys Club?
A: Elmer W. Welch in a home on High Street in 1897.

Q: When did Haverhill Boys Club become part of Boys Clubs of America
A: 1906.

Q: When did the Haverhill Girls Club start?
A: 1913.

Q: When were the first telephones in Haverhill installed?
A: 1877.

Q: What is the largest park in Haverhill?
A: Winnekenni.

Q: Where was the first post office in Haverhill?
A: Water Street (1775).

Q: In 1791, what was the public transportation to Boston?
A: Stage Coach.

Q: Name the first Haverhill built steamship to appear on the Merrimack River.
A: "Merrimack"

Q: In 1837, what new method of transportation was available from Bradford to Boston?
A: Train, however the railroad bridge to Haverhill was not built until 1839.

Q: Where in Haverhill is there a loom and spinning wheels?
A: Whittier's Birthplace.

Q: Where is there a collection of arrowheads and Indian artifacts found in Haverhill?
A: Buttonwoods Museum.

Q: "Indian Shutters" are wooden boards that slide across windows inside of a home for protection from arrows. Where in Haverhill can they be seen?
A: John Ward House

Q: Where in Haverhill can one find pictures of the 1936 flood?
A: Special Collections room- Haverhill Public Library

Q: Which park is the oldest in Haverhill?
A: G.A.R Park, formerly known as the common

Q: Name the oldest park in Bradford.
A: Bradford Common
Q: Where is the Haverhill Police Memorial?
A: Newcomb Street, side of City Hall

Q: Where is Hannah Duston buried?
A: No one knows for sure, but there are Dustons buried in Pentucket cemetery

Q: Who was the first Haverhill fire chief?
A: Ezekial Hale (1841-1845)

Q: Where is the Armenian Martyr's Monument in Haverhill?
A: In front of St. Gregory's Church, corner of Winter and Main Streets.

Q: Where is Haverhill is the "Worship Oak"?
A: Haverhill Historical Society - Buttonwoods Museum

Q: There are four mill stone markers in Haverhill. Where are they and why?
A: 1. Water Street-Landing site of first settlers.

2. Corner of Concord and Kenoza-Marks stage coach route to N.H

3. Near state rest area Rte.110 toward Methuen line. Marks site of Hannah Duston's return from captivity

4. Whitter Road- Marks site of John Greenleaf Whitter's schoolhouse

Q: The first monument to honor a woman (Hannah Duston) was repossessed for non-payment. Where is it now?
A: Barre, MA. It was a marble obelisk- now a Civil War Monument

Q: Where is the oldest living tree in New England?
A: At Buttonwoods. The "Worship Oak" believed to be 1000 years old.

Q: Name the parks and recreation areas of Haverhill.
A: Winnekenni Park - *Kenoza Ave*
Mount Washington Park
*Bradford Common - South Main St*
Swazey's Field - *Blaisdell and Marshall Streets*
G.A.R. Park - *Main St. and Winter St.*
River Rest Park - *Water Street*
Gale Park - *Kenoza and Mill Streets*
Twelfth Ave Playground
Riverside Park - *Lincoln Ave*
Plug Pond Recreation Area - *Mill St.*
Cashman Park - *Hilldale Ave*
The Promenade Deck -*Merrimack Street*
Columbus Park - *Railroad Ave*

Q: What is the item of clothing owned by the Haverhill Historical Society that is now in the Smithsonian Institute in Washington, D.C.?
A: A dress worn by Abigail Adams

Q: Where in Haverhill can you see a block of melted shoe nails from the "Great Fire" of 1882?
A: The Buttonwoods Museum

Q: Who was St. Crispin?
A: Patron Saint of Shoemakers

Q: The French Community donated a statue to the city in 1932. What is this statue?
A: General Lafayette - Lafayette Square

Q: What newspaper printed paper certificates to replace coins during the Civil War?
A: The Haverhill Gazette (1862). Metal was needed for the war effort.

Q: What is significant about the statue of George Washington at the Haverhill Public Library?
A: The statue of Washington was one of just two replicas that were cast from the original marble statue sculpted by the renowned French sculptor Jean-Antoine Houdon.

Q: What Haverhill citizen was the youngest major-general in the Civil War?
A: William Francis Bartlett. His statue is in the State House in Boston.

Q: Who was the Haverhill boy who overheard the British plan to go to Lexington and Concord and alerted General Warren?
A: William Baker

Q: Who was the first minister in Bradford?
A: Zachariah Symmes

Q: Who purchased Whittier's Birthplace for the city?
A: James H. Carleton (1818-1893)

Q: Who was the first Haverhill resident to sit on the Governor's Council?
A: Caleb Duston Hunking, shoe manufacturer and 2nd state senator, (1805-1872)

Q: Who hired Alexander Graham Bell to tutor his daughter and helped finance the telephone?
A: Thomas S. Sanders (1839-1911)

Q: Which Haverhill politician served as a State Representative and a Presidential Elector?
A: Rep. Francis J. Bevilacqua - voted for LBJ in 1964 Electoral College

Q: Who is credited with designing the City Seal?
A: James E. Gale, a member of the first City Council.

Q: Describe the City Seal:
A: It is a circle with Haverhill at the top, and a banner with "Pentucket" in it. Just below that is a crown signifying "Queen slipper city of the World". There is a shield, boot, an arm and hammer, and shoe. There is a sun rising between two hills, silver and golden. Advance of civilization is represented by a factory and two wigwams. An oak and laurel wreath are united below the seal, signifying strength and stability.Also present, "Settled"1640, Instituted as City 1870.

Q: What building in Bradford was a tavern and stage coach stop?
A: Kimball Tavern, built in 1692, Tavern from 1765-1830.

Q: Which mayor was the youngest appointed fire chief in Haverhill history?
A: Lewis Burton - Mayor 1976-1978

Q: Who was Bradford's first settler?
A: Robert Haseltine, who came from Rowley in 1649.

Q: Who was the Haverhill General who was president of the Court Martial which tried Benedict Arnold for treason?
A: General James Brickett

Q: Who was president of the Massachusetts Medical Society in 1867?
A: Dr. William Cogswell

Q: Which Haverhill business is the oldest family-owned pest control service in the U.S.?
A: Maguire Pest Control – Proprietor Dick "Bugger" Maguire – established 1905

Q: What clandestine Democratic political organization held meetings in Haverhill for over 50 years?
A: The Jackson Club

Q: Who started the first freight business to carry shoes from Haverhill to Boston and assisted making Haverhill widely known as an industrial city?
A: Rufus Slocumb

Q: Who was the assistant prosecutor in the Lizzy Borden Trial?
A: William H. Moody

Q: What was Lafayette Square called prior to 1900?
A: Sargeant Square.

Q: Who made a shell frame, preserved at Buttonwoods, while in prison during the Civil War?
A: William Griffin.

Q: Where is the Rocks Village hand pumper fire engine now located?
A: Ford Museum, Dearborn, Michigan.

Q: Mrs. Bixby of Haverhill lost five sons in the Civil War. She received a letter that can be seen at the Buttonwoods Museum. Who wrote the letter?
A: President Abraham Lincoln.

Q: Who was the first president of the Haverhill Historical Society? He was a man concerned with preserving our history.
A: Ira Abbott. (1845-1921)

Q: Name the Haverhill resident who was secretary to the man who would later become the second president of the United States.
A: John Thaxter, secretary to John Adams

Q: Name the woman who was captured by Indians and escaped by scalping her captors.
A: Hannah Duston in 1697

Q: Who was the physician, scientist, and author best known for building a castle?
A: Dr. James R. Nichols (1819 - 1888)

Q: Who was a Supreme Court Judge and Secretary of the Navy under President Theodore Roosevelt?
A: William H. Moody (1853 - 1917)

Q: Who was the citizen who owned a mill that made red flannel cloth and who funded the hospital and library for Haverhill's citizens?
A: Ezekial J.M. Hale (1813 – 1881)

Q: Who was Haverhill's Betsy Ross?
A: Nancy Buswell, a milliner who made a silk flag for the Hale Guards (Civil War). It can be seen at the Buttonwoods Museum. The flag was present at the Battle of Bull Run.

Q: Who was the Haverhill born surgeon who founded a famous clinic?
A: Dr. Frank Lahey (1880-1953)

Q: Name the Bradford man who had seven wives. Only the seventh wife outlived him.
A: Nathaniel Thurston, who is buried with six of his seven wives in the old Bradford burying ground.

Q: Who was the horticulturalist who developed the Bartlett Pear?
A: Enoch Bartlett (1779-1860)

Q: Name the Haverhill native who won the Congressional Medal of Honor under an assumed name.
A: George L. Day (1817 - 1921) Under the assumed name, John Mapes Adams

Q: What famous New York store was started in Haverhill?
A: Macy's Department Store

Q: Who offered the first money-back guarantee in America?
A: Rowland H. Macy

Q: Who was the Haverhill native who invented the photo finish camera for racetracks in 1936?
A: Harry I. Day

Q: Who invented the "burpless baby bottle", a collapsible, disposable baby bottle in 1959?
A: Inventor Grover Fitzgerald

Q: Who was the 18 year old boy who received the Carnegie Medal for heroism in 1925?
A: Albert Albanese, who attempted to save a 3 year old from the Merrimack River

Q: Who was King George's representative in Haverhill at the time of the American Revolution? He was a Tory who remained faithful to the king.
A: Colonel Richard Saltonstall.

Q: Which Haverhill nephew of John Adams had the solemn but noteworthy duty of conveying the 23rd Congress's condolences to Martha Washington at Mount Vernon upon the death of her husband George Washington and delivered their request that his remains be laid to rest in the city of Washington.
A: William Smith Shaw

Q: Who was the first female lawyer in Haverhill?
A: Mary Cavan (1885-1935)

Q: What Haverhill born man became the state senator, speaker of the House of Representatives, and later President of the Senate?
A: Leverett Saltonstall.

Q: Who is considered the "father" of Haverhill's shoe industry?
A: David How (1758-1842)

Q: Who was the Haverhill architect who designed Winnekenni and several buildings in the Washington Square district?
A: C. Willis Damon (He also designed City Hall, the Elks Home, and Wood, Knipe and Dyer Schools)

Q: Who was the first socialist elected mayor in the United States?
A: John C. Chase, Mayor of Haverhill

Q: Who was the first police officer in Haverhill?
A: Thomas Hale, appointed constable in 1648

Q: The Basiliere Bridge crosses the Merrimack River in Bradford. Who was Basiliere?
A: Ralph Basiliere, first Haverhill casualty of the Vietnam War

Q: Name the two Haverhill women who traveled to India as missionaries in the early nineteenth century.
A: Harriet Atwood Newell (1793-1812) and Ann Haseltine Judson (1789-1826)

Q: Who was the Countess?
A: Mary Ingalls of Haverhill, who married Count Francis de Vipart of France

Q: What Bradford man became a general in the Civil War?
A: General William Cogswell

Q: Western Electric and Bell Labs developed which important electronic component in the Winchell Building on Locust Street?
A: The transistor.

Q: Who made a shell frame, preserved at Buttonwoods, while in prison during the Civil War?
A: William Griffin

Q: What philanthropist funded the hospital and library for the good of Haverhill citizens and also paid for the statue of Hannah Duston?
A: Ezekial M Hale.

Q: Who traveled to the South Pole on an expedition with Admiral Byrd?
A: John Dyer.

Q: Name the first woman physician to practice in Haverhill. She was also among the first female physicians in the nation.
A: Dr. Debra Smith Drury (1824-1915) She graduated from medical school in 1860.

Q: Which Maine town was named after Haverhill native Col. Jonathan Buck?
A: Bucksport, ME

Q: Which Haverhill native was the first Greek woman in the U.S. to become a doctor?
A: Euterpe Dukakis

Q: Which Haverhill woman was the mother of a Democratic nominee for U.S. President?
A: Euterpe Dukakis

Q: Name the first black man who served Haverhill as both a policeman and a fireman.
A: Sydney Mason

Q: Who started the first bicycle shop in Haverhill?
A: Herbert R. Sawyer

Q: Name the international shoe designer who designed his first shoe at the age of 18 when his father sent him to work at a factory in Haverhill?
A: Stuart Weitzman

Q: Who was the last remaining survivor of the Armenian Genocide in Haverhill?
A: Jennie S. (Hekimian) Vartabedian 1911-2010

Q: Popular only in the Merrimack Valley, which card game was brought to Haverhill by Irish immigrants?
A: Forty-fives

Q: Which Haverhill native invented a hot water heating system fueled by coal or wood in 1887?
A: Noel Sawyer

## Math Trivia

1. If you commute to Boston 5 days per week to attend college and the distance is 33 miles from Haverhill, how many miles per week would you travel? -
Ans: 2 x 33 x 5 = 330 miles

2. You live one and a half miles from school. You walk to and from school five days per week. How many miles do you walk per week?
Ans. 15 miles

3. In 1940, Haverhill celebrated its tercentennary anniversary. How old was Haverhill then?
Ans. 300 years

4. If you walked to school one and a half miles at the rate of 1 mile in 12 minutes, how long would it take you to walk to school?
Ans.18 min.

5. What if you were walking with a friend at the same speed, how long would it take you?
Ans. 18 min.

6. There are 29,931 males in Haverhill and 32,442 females. How many more females than males?
Ans. 2,511

7. Haverhill became a city in 1870. How long has Haverhill been a city?
Ans. 142 years

8. In 1918, the Merrimack River froze. It was 20 degrees below zero. How many degrees below freezing was it?
Ans: 52 degrees

9. How long ago did the river freeze?
Ans. 94 years

10. Bradford was annexed to Haverhill in January, 1897. For how many years has Bradford been a part of Haverhill?
Ans. 115 years

*Photos courtesy of Brian Milewski*

# Can You Name And Locate The Following Scenes From Haverhill?

E. _____

I. _____

A. _____

B. _____

F. _____

J. _____

C. _____

G. _____

K. _____

D. _____

H. _____

L. _____

18

M. _____

R. _____

V. _____

N. _____

S. _____

W. _____

O. _____

X. _____

P. _____

T. _____

Y. _____

Q. _____

U. _____

Z. _____

# OPEN ENDED ACTIVITIES

1. Make a diorama of famous landmarks in Haverhill (buildings, monuments, etc.)

2. Make a calendar of important dates relative to Haverhill
   (Whittier'sbirthday, date of "Great Fire", birthday of the Countess, etc)

3. Design or upgrade a playground in Haverhill. Make a model of it.

4. Design a bumper sticker promoting Haverhill.

5. Design a new monument for the city. Where would it be? What does it
   commemorate?

6. Design a travel folder on Haverhill.

7. Write and videotape a 2 minute commercial promoting Haverhill. Attract tourists.

8. Haverhill does not have a motto. Write one.

9. Write a play dramatizing a historical event in our city's past.

10. Complete a book of trees found in our city (photographs, leaves, seeds).

11. Design a pamphlet "Who's who in Haverhill", containing current notable
    personalities.

12. Design a pamphlet on famous sons and daughters of Haverhill.

13. Draw a map of recreational areas in the city.

14. Compile a book on the monuments in the city. Include location, name, dates and
    what it commemorates.

15. Make models of bridges in Haverhill.

16. Make a model of Winnekenni Castle.

17. Make drawings of ships built in Haverhill.

18. Tape an interview with a senior citizen. Inquire about school, toys, jobs, clothing
    as a child, etc.

19. Research and write a report of George Washington's visit to the city. Compare
    Washington Square photos of the past to those of today.

20. Research the oldest part of a cemetery in your neighborhood. Do a rubbing of the
    most unusual headstone. Record oldest details.

21. Build a model of a "gundalow". Explain use.

22. Locate photos of trolley cars and electric cars in Haverhill. When did they begin
    and when did they end?

# OPEN ENDED ACTIVITIES

23. Research the oldest piece of fire apparatus in Haverhill. Interview the fire chief for information.

24. Research photographs of fire-fighting equipment. Make a photo time line of equipment to the present.

25. Write a report on the day the train fell off the bridge over Winter Street. Include photos from research.

26. Make a videotape tour of your school district.

27. Compile a list of sports figures from the city. Where are they now?

28. Research changes in bathing suits from mid 1800's to the present.

29. Trace your family back to its arrival in Haverhill.

30. Research the city emblem. Who designed it? What do the characters represent?

31. Visit Whittier's birthplace.
    Write "A Day in Your Life" on the farm during Whittier's boyhood.

32. Visit "Buttonwoods" home of Haverhill Historical Society. Bring your camera. Write a brochure to attract people to visit "Buttonwoods".

33. Design a set of "Who am I" cards.
    Clues on one side of card- picture and name, dates on opposite side.

34. Make a crossword puzzle based on Haverhill facts.

35. Make a Haverhill word search.

36. Write a song or poem about our city.

37. Choose an ethnic group in the city. Research and interview leaders to discover their contributions to the city.

38. Using a mortar and pestle or two flat stones, try to grind grain as the early settlers and Indians did.

39. In the spring, try maple sugaring. Keep a journal.

40. Choose a specific time-period. Research clothing of that time and dress figures in typical clothing of that era.

41. Keep a diary of all your activities for one day. List all of the things you would not have or could not have done if it were the year 1700.

42. Write a report on presidential visits to the city, names of presidents and dates of visits where possible.

# COLONIAL CAREERS FROM THE PAST

**Some early Haverhill jobs had unusual names.
Can you tell what each would do for work?**

| | | | | |
|---|---|---|---|---|
| a. | cordwainer | _____ | 1. | grinder of grain |
| b. | cooper | _____ | 2. | maker of men's hats |
| c. | wainwright | _____ | 3. | builder of houses |
| d. | miller | _____ | 4. | tavern owner |
| e. | tanner | _____ | 5. | a citizen; one who was at liberty |
| f. | husbandman | _____ | 6. | maker of men's clothes |
| g. | herdsman | _____ | 7. | maker of alcoholic beverages |
| h. | weaver | _____ | 8. | a barrel maker |
| i. | blacksmith | _____ | 9. | shoemaker |
| j. | merchant | _____ | 10. | a maker and dealer in tinware |
| k. | ordinary keeper | _____ | 11. | one who made items of silver |
| 1. | stiller | _____ | 12. | small land owner; farmer |
| m. | farrier | _____ | 13. | wagon repairman and wagon builder |
| n. | milliner | _____ | 14. | a maker of cloth |
| o. | housewright | _____ | 15. | trader; shopkeeper |
| p. | joiner | _____ | 16. | maker of women's hats |
| q. | turner | _____ | 17. | a maker of clothes and dealer in clothing |
| r. | yeoman | _____ | 18. | furniture maker |
| s. | tinker | _____ | 19. | one who worked with iron; maker of iron utensils |
| t. | clothier | _____ | 20. | a tiller of soil; farmer |
| u. | tinsmith | _____ | 21. | one who shod horses; at times a veterinarian |
| v. | hatter | _____ | 22. | one who turns wood; spindles, spokes, etc |
| w. | tailor | _____ | 23. | jack of all trades; mender of pots and kettles |
| x. | mariner | _____ | 24. | one who tended grazing animals |
| y. | silversmith | _____ | 25. | one who treated animal hides to make leather |
| z. | freeman | _____ | 26. | a crew member of a ship |

# MAPS OF HAVERHILL

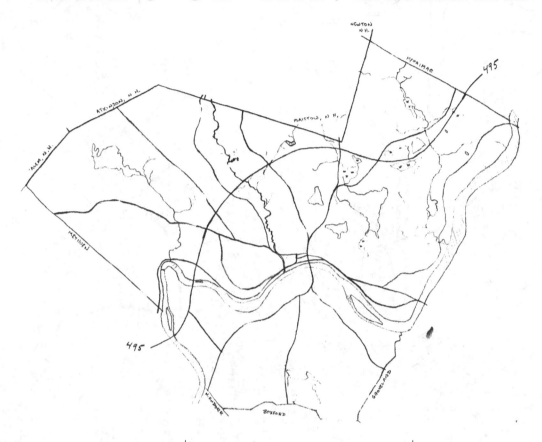

## Important Locations In Haverhill To Locate Or Identify:

1. Haverhill City Hall
2. Haverhill Historic Society (Buttonwoods Museum)
3. Haverhill Public Library
4. Dustin Garrison House
5. Northern Essex Community College
6. Whittier Homestead
7. Historic districts
   Washington Street
   Bradford Common
   Rocks Village
8. Your school
9. Winnekenni Castle

* Bonus Question:
   Every Dunkin' Donuts
   shop in Haverhill

## Major Roadways

1. Route 495
2. Route 110
3. Route 97
4. Route 108
5. Main Street
6. South Main Street
7. Washington Street
8. River Street
9. Water Street
10. Lincoln Ave
11. Broadway
12. East Broadway
13. North Broadway
14. Winter Street
15. Summer Street
16. Ginty Blvd.
17. Hilldale Ave
18. Monument Street
19. Mill Street

## Geographic Features

1. The Merrimack River
2. "Little River"
3. East Meadow River
4. Suicide Pond
5. West Meadow Brook
6. Millvale Reservoir
7. Kenoza Lake
8. Lake Saltonstall
9. Lake Pentucket
10. Crystal Lake
11. Chadwick Lake
12. Johnson's Pond
13. Ayer's Hill (Great Hill)
14. West Meadow Hill
15. Corliss Hill
16. Dead Hill
17. Silver Hill
18 Golden Hill
19. Ward Hill
20. Turkey Hill

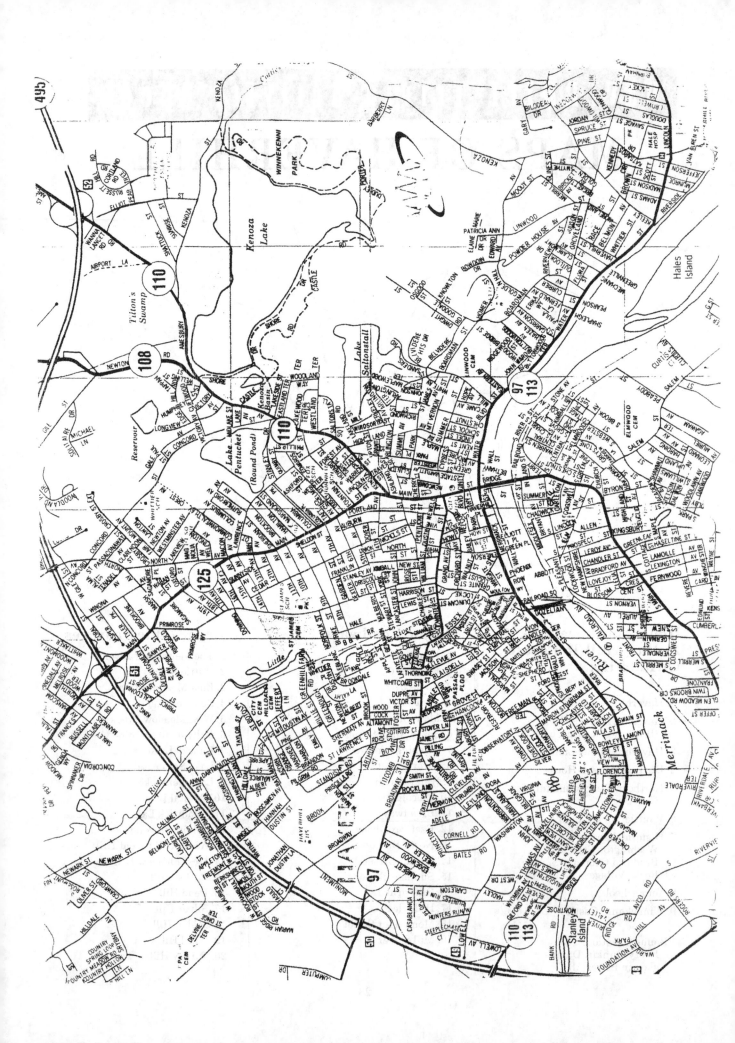

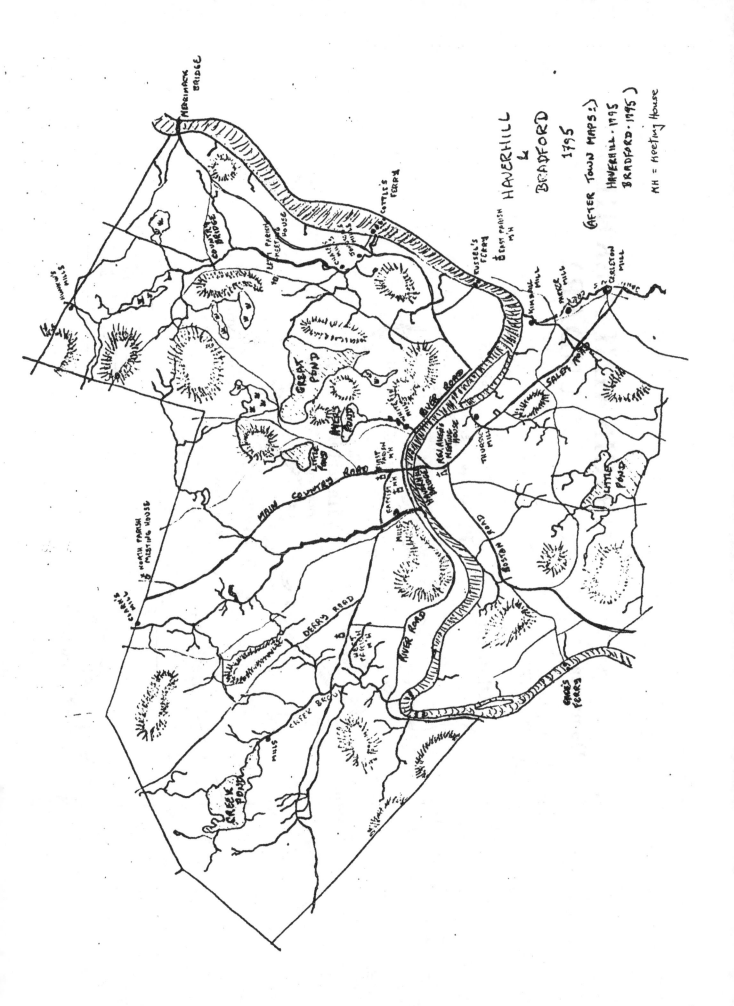

HAVERHILL
&
BRADFORD
1795

(AFTER TOWN MAPS:)

HAVERHILL · 1795
BRADFORD · 1795 )

MH = MEETING HOUSE

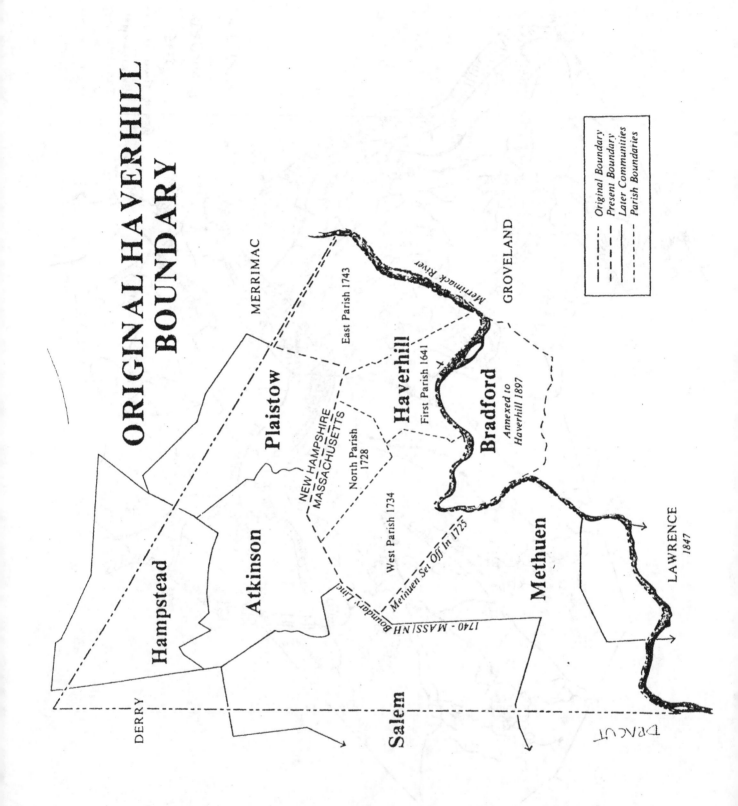

ORIGINAL HAVERHILL BOUNDARY

DERRY

Hampstead

Atkinson

Plaistow

NEW HAMPSHIRE
MASSACHUSETTS

MERRIMAC

East Parish 1743

North Parish 1728

Haverhill

First Parish 1641

Merrimack River

West Parish 1734

Methuen Set Off in 1725

1740 - MASS/NH Boundary Line

Salem

Bradford
Annexed to
Haverhill 1897

GROVELAND

Methuen

LAWRENCE
1847

DRACUT

Original Boundary
Present Boundary
Later Communities
Parish Boundaries

26

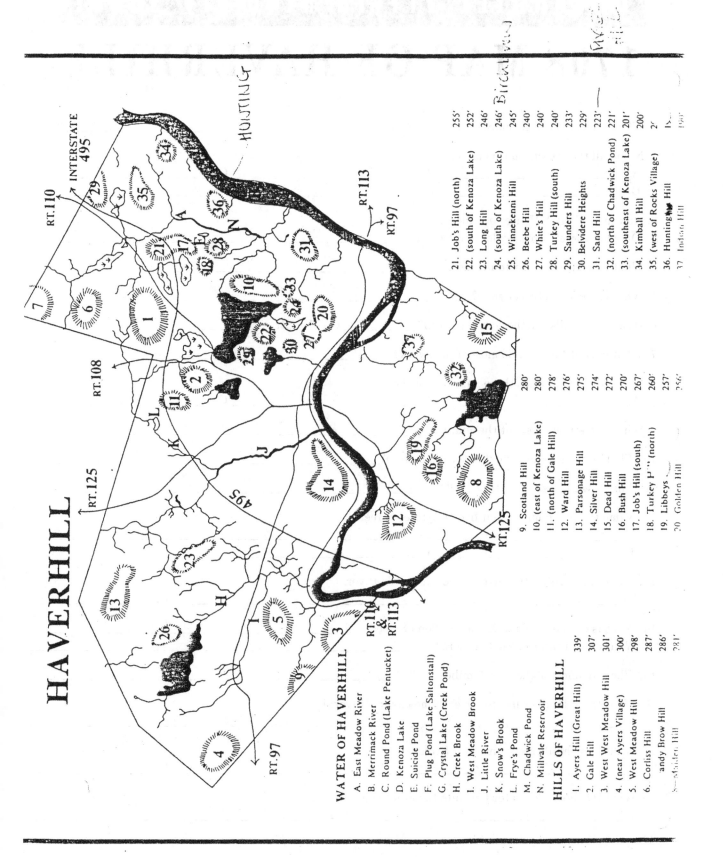

# HAVERHILL

RT.125
RT.110
RT.108
RT.97
495
RT.110 & RT.113
RT.113
RT.97
RT.125
INTERSTATE 495
HUNTING
Bridal way

## WATER OF HAVERHILL

A. East Meadow River
B. Merrimack River
C. Round Pond (Lake Pentucket)
D. Kenoza Lake
E. Suicide Pond
F. Plug Pond (Lake Saltonstall)
G. Crystal Lake (Creek Pond)
H. Creek Brook
I. West Meadow Brook
J. Little River
K. Snow's Brook
L. Frye's Pond
M. Chadwick Pond
N. Millvale Reservoir

## HILLS OF HAVERHILL

| 1. | Ayers Hill (Great Hill) | 339' |
| 2. | Gale Hill | 307' |
| 3. | West West Meadow Hill | 301' |
| 4. | (near Ayers Village) | 300' |
| 5. | West Meadow Hill | 298' |
| 6. | Corliss Hill | 287' |
| | andy Brow Hill | 286' |
| | Maiden Hill | 231' |

| 9. | Scotland Hill | 280' |
| 10. | (east of Kenoza Lake) | 280' |
| 11. | (north of Gale Hill) | 278' |
| 12. | Ward Hill | 276' |
| 13. | Parsonage Hill | 275' |
| 14. | Silver Hill | 274' |
| 15. | Dead Hill | 272' |
| 16. | Bush Hill | 270' |
| 17. | Job's Hill (south) | 267' |
| 18. | Turkey Hill (north) | 260' |
| 19. | Libbeys | 257' |
| 20. | Golden Hill | 256' |

| 21. | Job's Hill (north) | 255' |
| 22. | (south of Kenoza Lake) | 252' |
| 23. | Long Hill | 246' |
| 24. | (south of Kenoza Lake) | 246' |
| 25. | Winnekenni Hill | 245' |
| 26. | Beebe Hill | 240' |
| 27. | White's Hill | 240' |
| 28. | Turkey Hill (south) | 240' |
| 29. | Saunders Hill | 233' |
| 30. | Belvidere Heights | 229' |
| 31. | Sand Hill | 223' |
| 32. | (north of Chadwick Pond) | 221' |
| 33. | (southeast of Kenoza Lake) | 201' |
| 34. | Kimball Hill | 200' |
| 35. | (west of Rocks Village) | 2' |
| 36. | Hunting Hill | 1 |
| 37. | Indian Hill | 1 |

27

# 1708 MAP OF HAVERHILL

1. What is the title of the map? _____

2. Name all the streets on this map.
   A._____ B._____ C._____
   D._____ E._____ F._____

3. How many Watch Houses are there?_____
   On what streets are they located located? _____

4. What is next to the Duston House? _____

5. Where does Pond Street go to? _____

6. How many mills are there in Haverhill?_____ On Mill Street?_____

7. What part of the town do most of the Ayers live? _____

8. One body of water has three names. List them.
   A._____ B._____ C._____

9. What two streets meet at the church?_____

10. What body of water is next to the old church?_____

11. What town lies south of Haverhill?_____

12. Name the five families that live on Winter Street.
    1._____ 2._____ 3._____
    4._____ 5._____

13. Name the families that live west of the Little River.
    1._____ 2._____ 3._____ 4._____

14. What is on the corner of Main and Pond Street?_____
    What do you think is located there?_____

15. Where do most of the Ayer families live?_____

16. What three families live to the extreme east of Haverhill?
    1._____ 2._____ 3._____

17. What four families live on Water Street?
    1._____ 2._____ 3._____ 4._____

18. What two bodies of water flow into the Merrimack River?
    1._____ 2._____

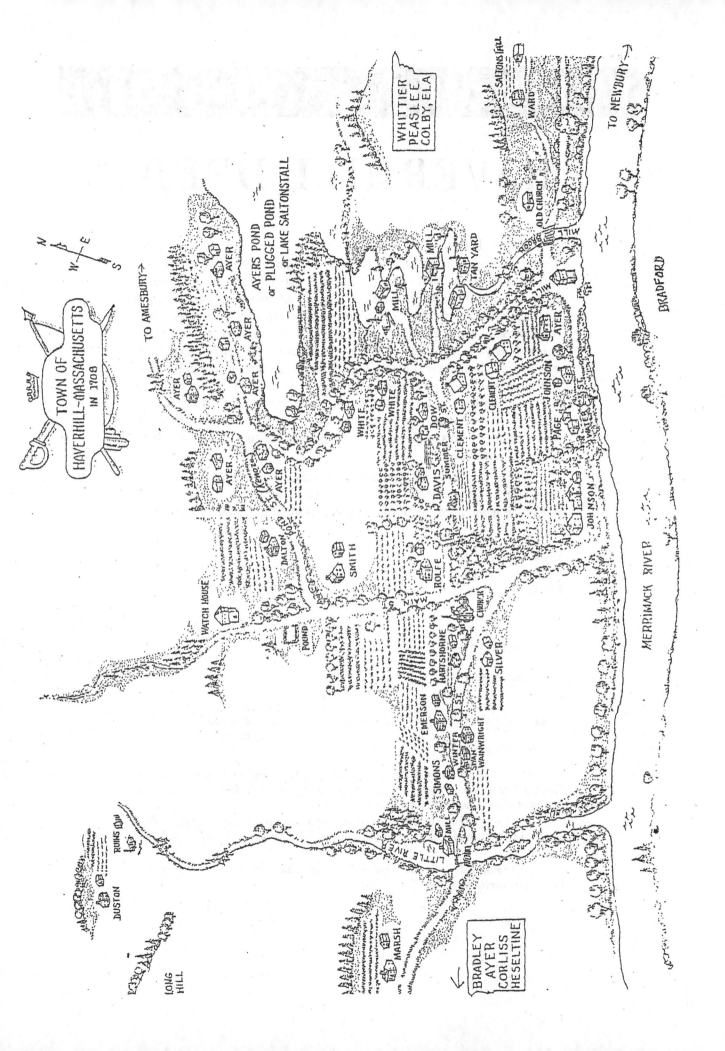

# HAVERHILL DEED

"Know all men by these presents, that wee Passaquo and S⁀⁀gaHew with ye consent of Passaconnaway; have sold unto ye inhabit⁀⁀ ⁀ Pentuckett all ye lands wee have in Pentuckett; that is eyght myle⁀ ⁀⁀ length from ye little Rivver in Pentuckett Westward: six myles in length from ye aforesaid Rivver northward: And six myles in length from ye aforesaid Rivver Eastward, with ye Ileand and ye rivver that ye ileand stand in as far in length as ye land lyes by as formerly expressed: that is, fourteen myles in length: And wee ye said Passaquo and SaggaHew with ye consent of Passaconaway, have sold unto ye said inhabitants all ye right that wee or any of us have in ye said ground and Ileand and Rivver: And wee warrant it against all or any other Indeans whatsoever unto ye said Inhabitants of Pentuckett, and to their heires and assignes forever Dated ye fifteenth day of november Ann Dom 1642.

Witnes our hands and seales to this bargayne of sale ye day and year above written (in ye presents of us,) wee ye said Passaquo & SaggaHew have received in hand, for & in consideration of ye same three pounds & ten shillings.

JOHN WARD

ROBERT CLEMENTS

TRISTRAM COFFIN

HUGH SHERRATT

WILLIAM WHITE

|  | | ye marke of |  |
| JOHN WARD | PASSAQUO | (A bow and arrow) | (Seal) |
|  |  | Passaquo |  |

ye signe of ( ᵢ )

THOMAS DAVIS

|  | | ye marke of |  |
| ye signe of ( ᵢ ) | SAGGAHEW | (A bow and arrow) | (Seal) |
|  |  | Saggahew |  |

*At the bottom the following is written:*—"Entered and recorded in ye County Records for Norfolk (lib. 2d, pa. 209) ye 29th day of April 1671 As attest Tho. Bradbury Recorder."

*On the side the following is written:*—"Recorded ye first of April 1681 among ye records of Lands for Essex at Ipswich: As attest Robert Lord Recorder."

*On the outside it is endorsed:*—"The purchase from the Indians by Haverhill men, Recorded."

# Haverhill Deed Activity Worksheet

## Vocabulary - Replace the old word spellings with modern terms

1. presents _____
2. ye _____
3. rivver _____
4. lyes _____
5. heires _____
6. bargayne _____

7. wee _____
8. marke _____
9. eyght _____
10. ileand _____
11. Indeans _____
12. seales _____

## Matching

A. Date the deed was signed
B. Chief of all the New England tribes
C. Who recorded the deed in Ipswich
D. Was witness to the deed signing
E. Where the deed was first recorded
F. Mark used by Passaquo and Sagghew
G. Original name of Haverhill on the deed
H. The date the deed first recorded
I. How much was paid for Pentucket
J. Who was the land sold to?
K. Names of the two Indians who sold Pentucket

_____ 1. Sagghew and Passaquo
_____ 2. April 29, 1671
_____ 3. Pentuckett
_____ 4. 3 Pounds Ten Schillings
_____ 5. November 15, 1642
_____ 6. Norfolk
_____ 7. Inhabitants of Pentucket
_____ 8. Tom Davis
_____ 9. Passaconway
_____ 10. Bow and Arrow
_____ 11. Robert Lord

How many square miles did the settlers purchase? _____

Name the settlers who signed the deed:

1._____
2._____
3._____
4._____
5._____

Name the the Indians who signed the deed:

1._____
2._____

Knowe all men by thefe prſents that wee : Paſſaquo : and Sagga Hew, wᵗʰ the conſent of Paſſaconnaway : haue ſold vnto the the Inhabitants of Pentuckett all the lands we haue in Pentucket ; that is Eyght myles in lenght from the little Riuer in Pentuckett weſtward : Six miles in lenght frō the aforeſaid Riuer northward : And Six miles in lenght frō the foreſaid Riuer Eſtward wᵗʰ the Ileland and the Riuer that the Ileland ſtand in as far in lenght as the land lyes by in formerly expreſſed, that is, fourteene myles in lenght : And wee the ſaid Paſſaquo & Saggahew wᵗʰ the conſent of Paſſaconnaway haue ſold vnto the ſaid Inhabitants all the Right that wee or any of vs haue in the ſaid ground Ileland & Riuer : And Doe warrant it againſt all or any other Indeans whatſoeū vnto the ſaid Inhabitants of Pentuckett & to there heyres and aſſignes for euer Dated the fifteenth Day of nouember Ann Dom 1642.

witneſ ouʳ hands & ſeales to this bargayne of ſale the Day & yere aboue written in the prſents of vs : wee the ſaid Paſſaquo & Saggahew haue Receiued in hand for & in conſideracon of the ſame three pounds & ten ſhillings

Jᴏʜɴ Wᴀʀᴅ                              the marke of
Rᴏʙᴇʀᴛ Cʟᴇᴍᴇɴᴛs
Tʀɪsᴛʀᴀᴍ Cᴏғғʏɴ        Pᴀssᴀǫᴜᴏ          [ꜱᴇᴀʟ]
Hᴇᴜɢʜ Sʜᴇʀʀᴀᴛᴛ
Wɪʟʟɪᴀᴍ ᴡʜɪᴛᴇ                       The marke of
    The ſigne of
Tʜᴏᴍᴀs 🕮 Dᴀᴜɪᴄᴇ Sᴀɢɢᴀʜᴇᴡ :              [ꜱᴇᴀʟ]

# WINNEKENNI CASTLE

- ## THE FIRST FLOOR

- Has a library measuring 12 x 16 feet.

- A formal reception room 22 x 31 feet.

- The middle of this room, was a stairway, that led up to the second floor. It was 70 feet long.

- ## THE SECOND FLOOR:

- The 16x18 master bedroom is located here, then 4 minor bedrooms, 12 x 12 , and 4 smaller guest rooms 8 x 8.

- There were 51 separate windows throughout the castle.

- All the rooms had hardwood floors except the large reception room that had a marble floors, and contained black mahogany furniture.

- ## OUTSIDE THE CASTLE:

- Tennis courts, court yard, croquet yard, a boat house, beautiful gardens all over the castle grounds, and surrounding acres of woods for recreation.

## FACTS ABOUT THE CASTLE

- 1696 - John guild pays 50 pounds for the side hill near Kenoza Lake.

- 1807 - People purchase land for a summer resort, they build wooden huts along the lake and basin.

- 1859- Kenoza Lake was originally known as "Great Pond", being renamed by John Greenleaf Whittier as "Kenoza Lake", which means "Lake of the Pickerel".

- 1872 - Dr. James Nichols builds a castle on the top of the hill near the basin.

Here's a description of the castle he built:

The walls are 4 feet thick.

Two of the walls are 86 feet long, the other two are 36 feet wide.

A stable near the castle was 400 feet square.

Four towers on each end of the walls are 55 feet high.

There is a large gothic door as the main entrance to the castle. As you enter through the door, you come to a small reception hall that is 12 x 16 feet.

- 1878 - Dr. Darling builds a summer cottage near the shore line.

# Winnekenni Castle Activity Worksheet

1. Kenoza Lake is next to a _____
   The Indians referred to it as the _____
   In _____ John _____ paid _____ pounds for the hill near _____

2. The first floor consisted of how many rooms? _____
   List the names of the rooms on the first floor? _____
   Was there a kitchen on the first floor?_____
   What started on the first floor and ended up on the second floor? _____
   How long is this object? _____

3. Which floors were made of marble? _____
   What kind of floors were in the rest of the castle? _____
   Did the Castle have towers? _____ How many? _____ How high are they? _____

4. Name the things that were found on the outside of the castle? _____
   _____
   _____

5. How many separate windows are in the castle?_____
   What kind of wood was the furniture made from? _____
   How many bedrooms located on the first floor? _____
   How many bedrooms located on the? _____
   Which was the biggest bedroom? _____ How many square feet? _____
   How much was the square footage in the guest rooms? _____
   How many square feet in the minor bedrooms? _____
   In the reception hall? _____
   How thick are the walls? _____ How long? _____Wide? _____
   Square footage of the first floor? _____

6. When were wooden huts built along the basin? _____
   Who had the first summer cottage? _____

7. What kind of doors were found at the main entrance? _____
   Was there a porch? _____

8. What outside the Castle was four hundred square feet? _____
   When was the castle begun? _____

# BOSTON & MAINE RAILWAY

1) What is the month and year for the train schedule?

   _____

2) How many stops between Boston, MA and Portland, ME?

   _____

3) What are the three branches are shown in the schedule?

   _____

4) What is the farthest northwest stop on the railroad line?

   _____

5) Who is the passenger agent listed?

   _____

6) How would you take a train to get to Boston from Haverhill?

   _____

7) What time did the 9:32 am train from Bradford arrive in Reading?

   _____

8) Who was the B&M Railroad President?

   _____

9) What time did the Alton Bay 3:45 pm train arrive in Boston?

   _____

10) How would B&M get you to Wolfeboro from Alton Bay?

   _____

## 45   BOSTON AND MAINE RAILWAY.

F. COGSWELL, President,       Boston, Mass.
W. BLANCHARD, Treasurer.
W. MERRITT, Gen. Superintendent.
J. S. EATON, Gen. Ticket Agent.
J. B. GILLETT, Jr., Gen. Freight Agent.
A. ROWE, Passenger Agent.

M. E. WOOD, Pass. Trans. Master at Boston Pass.
    Station, and Purchasing Agent, Boston, Mass.
D. HASTY, Freight Agent,     Lawrence, Mass.
M. G. GALE, Master Mechanic,    Boston, Mass.
D. C. RICHARDSON, Master Car Builder,
                     Lawrence, Mass.

**May, 1870.**

An additional train leaves Boston for North Lawrence at 10.15 a.m., arriving there 11.25 a.m. Leave North Lawrence at 12.15 and 5.30 p.m., arriving in Boston at 1.15 and 6.26 p.m.

The 6.00 p.m. express train from Boston to South Berwick Junction, and the 7.25 p.m. train from South Berwick Junction run Monday, Wednesday and Friday only.

STANDARD OR TRUE—Clock in Passenger Station at Boston.

## BOSTON AND MAINE RAILWAY,
### BRANCHES, &c.

**46**    NEWBURYPORT RAILWAY.    May, 1870.

**47**    DOVER AND WINNIPISEOGEE RAILWAY.    May, 1870.

Stages leave Alton daily on arrival of the morning train from Dover, for Wolfboro, connecting there on Tuesdays, Boston, and Portland, and Saturdays, with Stages for Tuftonborough, Sandwich, &c. Also leave Alton for Laconia, Tuesdays, Thursdays & Saturdays. Stages leave Laconia for Alton, Mondays, Wednesdays and Fridays.

**48½** Haverhill & Georgetown Trains.—Leave Haverhill 6.15, 7.30, 9.30, 11.00 a.m., & 4.00, 5.00, 6.05 & 7.15 p.m. Returning, leave Georgetown at 6.35, 7.50, 9.08, 11.20 a.m., and 4.36, 5.35, 6.35 and 7.40 p.m.

## CONNECTIONS OF BOSTON AND MAINE RAILWAY.

1 With Railways diverging from Boston.
2 With South Reading Branch.
3 With Salem and Lowell Railway.
4 With Lowell and Lawrence Railway.
5 With Manchester and Lawrence Railway.
6 With Newburyport Railway.
7 With Concord and Portsmouth Railway.
8 With Dover and Winnipisseogee Railway.
9 With Portsmouth, Great Falls and Conway Railway.
* With Portland, Saco and Portsmouth Railway.
10 With Railways East from Portland.
11 With Salem and Lowell Railway.
12 With Eastern Railway, Mass.

MAP OF THE BOSTON & MAINE RAILWAY & CONNECTIONS

# HAVERHILL FOOD TRIVIA QUIZ

1)      How many supermarkets are in Haverhill?

2)      What is the name of the pizza shop on White St. known for its rectangular shaped slices?

3)      What national coffee chain is at the corner of Main and Rosemont?

4)      What is the name of the chicken restaurant on Broadway?

5)      Which Chinese restaurant has two locations in Haverhill?

6)      What is the name of the sandwich that Benedetti's Deli sells?

7)      What is the name of the breakfast place in Bradford Square?

8)      How many McDonald's are there in Haverhill/Bradford?

9)      Which restaurant sells Indian style food on Merrimack Street?

10)     What is the name of the deli on Merrimack Street near the Landmark Building?

11)     Name three restaurants on Washington Street.

12)     What national pizza chains are in Haverhill?

13)     Name the seafood restaurant at the corner of Winter and Emerson.

14)     Name three ice cream stands in Haverhill/Bradford.

15)     Name a donut shop in Haverhill other than Dunkin Donuts.

# HAVERHILL SCHOOLS WORD SEARCH

```
E H S X D M D G P G T E G H M
Q K N I O R N S R O R T O G W
U F A O L I O E H A J I L I T
O L D L K V E F U H I L D H T
Z Y I N T N E Q D H R T E L E
G B U Z L E S R H A I O N L L
B H G E T T K N H M R N H I T
K L A A U M Y C E I A B I H R
Q F T N I Q W B U T L R L R A
B M L X A O O C P T T L L E B
U A R E I T T I H W N L K V K
W C O N S E N T I N O E E A P
C R O W E L L K Z P D I P H P
W N E M B M V D R E H L W V Z
I M H Z R W D R G M O S C X J
```

| BARTLETT | GREENLEAF | PENTUCKETLAKE |
|----------|-----------|---------------|
| BRADFORD | HAVERHILLHIGH | SILVERHILL |
| CONSENTINO | HUNKING | TILTON |
| CROWELL | MOODY | WALNUTSQUARE |
| GOLDENHILL | NETTLE | WHITTIER |

# ARCHIE COMICS ACTIVITY

1.    Who wrote Archie comics?

2.    What is it based on?

3.    What evidence is there of that?

4.    Where does Archie live?

5.    What is his best friend's name?

6.    What are the names of the two girls who fight over Archie?

7.    Which girl is the rich one?

8.    Which one is down to earth, girl next door?

9.    Whom does Archie finally marry?

10.    What is the principal's name?

# HAVERHILL HISTORY CROSSWORD

**Across:**

1. Bradford Native American tribe
3. Haverhill's first police officer
6. Native American tribe that captured Hannah Duston
7. Haverhill's first street
8. Native America word meaning pickerel
9. Religion of English settlers

12. Original water supply of settlers
15. Native American's name meaning place of the winding river

**Down:**

2. Bradford's first minister
4. Native American word for very beautiful
5. Oldest street in Bradford
9. Haverhill Native American tribe
10. This town was originally part of Bradford
11. Bradford was originally part of this town
13. Haverhill's first minister

14. Name for fish traps that were used in Little River
16. Bradford's first settler
17. Flat bottomed barge used for transporting hay and goods on Merrimack River

## Colonial Careers Answer Key

1. D. cordwainer - shoemaker
2. V. cooper - barrel maker
3. O. wainwright - wagon repairman and wagon builder
4. K. miller - grinder of grain
5. Z. tanner - one who treated animal hides to make leather
6. W. husbandman - a tiller of the soil; farmer
7. L. herdsman - one who tended grazing animals
8. B. weaver - a maker of cloth
9. A. blacksmith - one who worked with iron; maker of iron utensils
10. U. merchant - trader; shopkeeper
11. Y. ordinary keeper - tavern owner
12. R. stiller - maker of alcoholic beverages
13. C. farrier - one who shod horses; at times a veterinarian
14. H. milliner - maker of women's hats
15. J. housewright - builder of houses
16. N. joiner - furniture maker
17. T. turner - one who turns wood; spindles, spokes etc.
18. P. yeoman - small land owner; farmer
19. I. tinker - jack of all trades; mender of pots and kettles
20. F. clothier - a maker of clothes and dealer in clothing
21. M. tinsmith - a maker and dealer in tinware
22. Q. hatter - maker of men's hats
23. S. tailor - maker of men's clothes
24. G. mariner - a crew member on a ship
25. E. silversmith - one who made items of silver
26. X. freeman - a citizen; one who was at liberty

---

## Boston & Maine Railway Answer Key

1. May 1870
2. 28
3. Boston and Maine Railway, Newburyport Railway, Dover and Winnipissocke Railway
4 Alton Bay
5. A. Rowe
6. Go to Haverhill Depot on Railroad Ave.
7. 10:10 am
8. F. Coggswell
9. 8:00 pm
10. Stage Coach

## HAVERHILL HISTORY CROSSWORD PUZZLE KEY
Please complete the crossword puzzle below

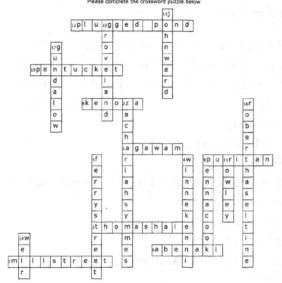

**Across:**

1. Bradford Native American tribe (agawam)
3. Haverhill's first police officer (thomashale)
6. Native American tribe that captured Hannah Duston (abenaki)
7. Haverhill's first street (millstreet)
8. Native America word meaning pickerel (kenoza)
9. Religion of English settlers (puritan)
12. Original water supply of settlers (plugged pond)
15. Native American's name meaning place of the winding river (pentucket)

**Down:**

2. Bradford's first minister (zachariahsymmes)
4. Native American word for very beautiful (winnekenni)
5. Oldest street in Bradford (ferrystreet)
9. Haverhill Native American tribe (pennacook)
10. This town was originally part of Bradford (groveland)
11. Bradford was originally part of this town (rowley)
13. Haverhill's first minister (johnward)
14. Name for fish traps that were used in Little River (weir)
16. Bradford's first settler (roberthaseltine)
17. Flat bottomed barge used for transporting hay and goods on Merrimack River (gundalow)

## Word Search Solution

```
E + S + D M + G + G + E G H +
+ K + I O R N + R + R T O G +
+ + A O L I O E + A + I L I T
+ + D L K V E F U + + L D H T
+ Y + N T N E Q D + + T E L E
+ + U + L E S R + A + O N L L
+ H + E + T K N H + R N H I T
+ + A + U + + C E I + B I H R
+ F + N + + + + U T L + L R A
+ + L + + + + + + T T L L E B
+ A R E I T T I H W N L + V +
W C O N S E N T I N O E E A +
C R O W E L L + + + + + P H +
+ + + + + + + + + + + + + + +
+ + + + + + + + + + + + + + +
```

(Over,Down,Direction)
BARTLETT(15,10,N)
BRADFORD(12,8,NW)
CONSENTINO(2,12,E)
CROWELL(1,13,E)
GOLDENHILL(13,1,S)
GREENLEAF(10,1,SW)
HAVERHILLHIGH(14,13,N)
HUNKING(2,7,NE)
MOODY(6,1,SW)
NETTLE(8,7,SE)
PENTUCKETLAKE(13,13,NW)
SILVERHILL(3,1,SE)
TILTON(12,2,S)
WALNUTSQUARE(1,12,NE)
WHITTIER(10,11,W)

## HAVERHILL FOOD TRIVIA QUIZ
### Answer Key

1. 4 – Three Market Baskets, BJ's Wholesale
2. Napoli's Pizza
3. Starbucks Coffee
4. Chicken Connection
5. Oriental Gardens
6. The Rocket
7. Village Square
8. 3- S. Main Bradford, River Street, N. Main St.
9. Royal India
10. A-1 Deli
11. Artist Café, Blue Finn Grille, Keon's 105, OG2, The Tap, the Lasting Room, Toma's, Barking Dog Ale House, Andino's Italian Kitchen, Mark's Deli
12. Papa Gino's, Domino's
13. Bradford Seafood
14. Carters, Biggarts, Burke's, Moo-Moos, Crescent Farms
15. Heavn'y Donuts

## ARCHIE COMICS QUIZ
### Answer Key

1. Bob Montana
2. Haverhill High School
3. Thinker statue and Brown & Gold school colors
4. Riverdale
5. Jughead Jones
6. Betty Cooper and Veronica Lodge
7. Veronica Lodge
8. Betty Cooper
9. Veronica then Betty (Long story)
10. Waldo Weatherbee

## WINNEKENNI WORKSHEET
### Answer Key

1. Basin
   Great Pond - Lake of the Pickerel
   1696
   Guild
   50 pounds
   Kenoza Lake

2. Two Rooms
   Library and Reception
   No Kitchen on the first floor
   Stairway
   70 ft
   Reception room has marble floors
   Hardwood

3. Yes
   Four towers
   55 ft. high

4. Tennis courts, court yard, croquet yard, boat house, gardens, woods

5. 51 windows
   black mahogany
   0, no first floor bedrooms
   9
   master bedroom, 288 sq. ft
   64 sq. ft Guest Rooms
   144 sq.ft Minor Bedroom
   682 sq ft Reception Hall
   4 ft. thick, 86 ft. long, 36 ft.wide
   874 sq. ft

6. 1807
   Dr. Darling

7. Gothic doors
   No porch

8. Stables
   1872

## 1708 MAP OF HAVERHILL ACTIVITY
### Answer Key

1. Town of Haverhill Massachusetts In 1708
2. Winter, Main, Pond, Mill, Water, Summer
3. 2 Watch Houses – North Main St., Mill St.
4. Ruins
5. Amesbury
6. 3 Mills – Two on Mill St.
7. Northeast
8. Ayers Pond, Plugged Pond, Lake Saltonstall
9. Main and Winter
10. Mill Brook
11. Bradford
12. Simons, Swan, Wainwright, Emerson, Silver,
13. Bradley, Ayer, Corliss, Heseltine
14. Pound
15. Northeast
16. Whittier, Peaslee, Colby, Ela
17. Johnson, Page, Johnson, Ayer
18. Little River, Mill Brook

## HAVERHILL DEED ACTIVITY
### Answer Key

| Vocabulary | Matching | Square Miles? 42 |
|---|---|---|
| 1. presence | 1. K | Area of a triangle: |
| 2. the | 2. H | $1/2$ B x H |
| 3. river | 3. G | B=14: |
| 4. lies | 4. I | 8 mi. West + 6 mi. East of |
| 5. heirs | 5. A | Little River = 14 mi. |
| 6. bargain | 6. E | |
| 7. we | 7. J | H=6: |
| 8. mark | 8. D | 6 mi. North of Little River |
| 9. eight | 9. B | |
| 10. island | 10. F | |
| 11. Indians | 11. C | |
| 12. seals | | |

1. John Ward
2. Robert Clements
3. Tristam Coffin
4. Hugh Sherratt
5. William White

1. Passaquo
2. Saggahew

# Locate & Name This Place Answer Key

A. Haverhill Fire Department Credit Union (former Armory), Kenoza Avenue

B. Haverhill City Hall, Summer Street

C. Duston Garrison House, Hilldale Avenue

D. Haverhill District Court House – Bailey Boulevard

E. Buttonwoods - Haverhill Historical Society, Water Street

F. Firemen's Memorial Statue, Linwood Cemetery, Mill Street

G. Dudley Porter Memorial, Winnekenni Park

H. Post Office, Washington Square

I. Winnekenni Castle, Kenoza Avenue

J. Powder House, Golden Hill Avenue

K. Walnut Square School, Main Street

L. Hannah Duston Statue, G.A.R. Park

M. Whittier's Birthplace, Whittier Road

N. Civil War Monument, Monument Square

O. Merrimack Valley Hospital, Lincoln Avenue

P. Universalist Unitarian Church of Haverhill, Ashland Street

Q. Water Street Fire Station, Water Street

R. Ayers Village Fire Station

S. "The Hiker" Spanish-American War Memorial, Gale Park

T. Kimball's Tavern, Salem Street

U. Lafayette Statue, Lafayette Square

V. Haverhill Police Department, Ginty Boulevard

W. First Church of Christ, Church Street

X. All Saints Parish, Broadway

Y. John Ward House, Water Street

Z. Rocks Village Fire Station, Merrimac Road

44

# Haverhill, Massachusetts TRIVIA BOOK

## Haverhill Citizens Hall of Fame

One measure of the nature of a community is the caliber of the people it produces or significantly influences.

The sons and daughters of Haverhill who have achieved a significant degree of fame range from a world famous poet to a colonial heroine; from a motion picture mogul to a physician whose name remains internationally known for medical diagnosis and treatment. Included are persons in military, government and scientific fields.

The Hall of Fame was dedicated on March 6,1986, with Governor Michael S. Dukakis as the principal speaker. Other speakers have included former Secretary of Defense Dick Cheney, who later went on to become vice president of the United States; former Governor John A. Volpe; and Deputy Secretary of Defense Donald J. Atwood, who was later inducted into the Hall of Fame in his own right.

An explanation of the Hall of Fame comes from the dedication plaque:

*"The Haverhill Citizens Hall of Fame was established at the Haverhill Public Library in 1985. Its purpose is to recognize, prominently and permanently, individuals from Haverhill who have made significant contributions to the larger communities of state, country and world, of which we are all citizens.*

*'This Hall of Fame, by calling attention to the part that Haverhill has played in the lives of these individuals, will serve as a source of pride and inspiration and will provide an opportunity for future generations to better understand their community's history."*

The major criteria are that the individual must have had a "substantive Haverhill connection," that they have had a "significant impact beyond Haverhill's borders," and that, to allow for the assessment of time, must be deceased.

On the pages that follow are the members of the Haverhill Citizens Hall of Fame, in order of induction.

## John Greenleaf Whittier *1807-1892*

Mr. Whittier was one of the most prominent natives of Haverhill, gaining national and international fame through his poetry. His earlier fame, however, came through his opposition to slavery, a crusade that led to the Civil War and the elimination of slavery.

He was born in 1807 to a Quaker family in a farmhouse that remains to this day a true literary shrine, preserved as it was when he lived there.

His poetry that brought him acclaim is still being read and recited. He has been enshrined in the Poets Corner of the Cathedral of St. John the Divine in New York City.

A city and a college were named for him in California and his poetry is still being quoted, in books, in schools, even on television. He died in 1892 and is buried in Amesbury

## Hannah Emerson Dustin *1657-1732*

Hannah Dustin was the first woman in this country to have a statue created and erected in her honor.

This was because she became a historic colonial figure in 1697 when she was captured by a Native American raiding party, her baby was killed and she was taken north into New Hampshire.

She escaped and killed several of her captors in doing so. Her adventure attracted much attention. She was admired by many but also criticized by many for the way she escaped.

The statue depicting her historic episode overlooks downtown Haverhill GAR Park. Her descendants have created a widespread family association throughout the country.

## Frank Howard Lahey *1880-1953*

The medical clinic Dr. Lahey established in Burlington had achieved international renown even while he was still practicing as a surgeon in addition to his administration work.

He was born in a house at Primrose and Charles streets in 1880, and after graduating from Haverhill High School in 1900, he went on to Harvard to start his medical career.

His prominence as a doctor led to his election as president of the American Medical Association in 1942, and he was head of the Army and Navy Procurement Board in World War II.

He was a leader in the fields of thyroid diseases, medical education, surgical techniques and anesthesia and a pioneer in surgical procedures.

## William H. Moody *1853-1917*

A distinguished law and political career took Mr. Moody from his law office in Haverhill to national prominence.

He was a prosecutor at the sensational murder trial of Lizzie Borden. He was elected to Congress in 1895, and resigned in 1902 to become Secretary of the Navy. He later became the Attorney General of the United States from 1904 to 1906, when he was named to the Supreme Court.

He was on the Supreme Court until 1910 when he retired because of ill health. He lived until 1917 in the house at 38 Saltonstall Road that was built for him in 1900.

The Moody School on Margin Street was named for him.

## Thomas S. Sanders *1839-1911*

Mr. Sanders was a successful leather merchant in Haverhill, after making a significant change in processing, when he hired Alexander Graham Bell to tutor his deaf mute son.

He became interested in Bell's experiments with sound transmission and eventually became the chief financial backer in the development of the telephone.

As a result, Mr. Sanders became the first treasurer of Bell Telephone. The first public use of the telephone in Haverhill was from City Hall to Mr. Sanders' home at 169 Kenoza Ave., June 4, 1877.

He later built a sumptuous home, "Birchbrow," overlooking Lake Saltonstall (Plug Pond) where he lived until his death. The fashionable house was destroyed by fire several years ago.

## James Brickett *1738-1818*

Dr. Brickett's distinguished military career started as a surgeon during the French and Indian Wars. He was a captain in the Haverhill Artillery Company and led troops to the Battle of Bunker Hill, where he was wounded.

He advanced through the ranks to Brigadier General in the Revolution, and fought in the "sea battle" on Lake Champlain.

He guarded British General Burgoyne and his surrendered troops in Vermont, and finally escorted them back to Boston to their ships, to return to England. He returned to his home on the north side of Water Street until his death in 1818.

## Louis B. Mayer *1885 - 1957*

When he came to Haverhill from St. John, New Brunswick, Louis Mayer was in the unglamorous business of dealing in junk.

However, he was quick to realize the potential of the new motion picture business and he brought his first theater on Essex Street with borrowed money. He soon was able to build his own theatre on Merrimack Street, and from there the path led to California.

In Hollywood, Mr. Mayer eventually became one of the most powerful men in the movie industry, as a co-founder of Metro-Goldstein studios and the originator of the star system. The star system was the method of creating, promoting and exploiting movie stars in Classical Hollywood cinema.

He made a triumphant return to Haverhill in 1955 as the guest at Greater Haverhill Chamber of Commerce dinner.

## Bailey Bartlett *1750 - 1830*

From his base in Haverhill as a merchant dealing in English goods, Mr. Bartlett moved in government circles to take part in some of the most historic moments in early life of this country.

He was a friend of John and Samuel Adams and was with them in Philadelphia when the Declaration of Independence was signed.

He was a member of the convention that ratified the U.S. Constitution.

In 1797, he was elected to Congress and was at the last session to be held in Philadelphia and the first in Washington D.C.

## James U. Crockett *1915-1979*

Millions of television viewers got acquainted with this 1933 graduate of Haverhill High School when National Public Television picked up the program that started at Boston's Channel 2, WGBH. It was titled "Crockett's Victory Garden."

He began his career in gardening at the Gray & Cole Nursery in Ward Hill and studied horticulture at the Stockbridge, Mass., School of Agriculture and Texas A&M University.

He wrote 18 books and numerous newspaper and magazine articles.

He was awarded the Mass. Horticultural Society's George Robert White Medal of Honor in 1979.

## Bob Montana *1920-1975*

The world-famous comic strip character of "Archie" and all his high school companions emerged from the halls of Haverhill High School, where artist Bob Montana said he spent the three best years of his young life.

He was born into a vaudeville and theater family, but his talent for drawing and wry comedy soon became evident, and he was the foremost illustrator of the school's newspaper and yearbook in his generation.

After his service in World War II, the people he created became known everywhere through newspapers and magazines, and the legacy of Bob Montana and Archie became one of the mainstays of the popular comic publishing business.

When he succumbed to a heart attack in 1975, he left many to wonder about the real people on whom he based his characters.

## John C. Chase *1870-?*

When Mr. Chase was elected mayor of Haverhill in 1898, he became the first socialist to serve as mayor of an American city.

He was born in Gilmanton, N.H., but became a shoemaker in Haverhill in 1882 and joined the trade union movement in 1886.

He was re-elected mayor in 1899 and became the chairman of the national convention of the Social Democratic Party in 1901.

He was a candidate for the governor of Massachusetts, and also of New York; he became a national officer of the Socialists in 1908, and later was Nebraska state secretary

He was a candidate for Congress from West Virginia in 1922, 1924, and 1934.

No one in Haverhill has been able to learn the date and place of his death.

## William Francis Bartlett *1840-1876*

An outstanding military record in the civil war led to Mr. Bartlett becoming the youngest Major General in the Union Army at the age of 25

He achieved that honor when he returned to duty after losing a leg to wounds in the siege of Yorktown.

He had entered the Army after graduating from Harvard, and was appointed a captain of the 20th Mass, Infantry.

He led Union forces at Petersburg where he was captured and held in a confederate prison until the war ended. A full-length statue was placed in the State House in 1904.

## Stuart Chase *1888-1985*

Mr. Chase, an economist, was raised mainly in Haverhill, but after he attended MIT and Harvard, he soon went to Washington D.C, where his work with the government started World War I.

He is credited with coining the name of "The New Deal" for the presidency of Franklin D. Roosevelt, who took the name from the title of Mr. Chase's first book, "A New Deal."

He later became one of the first members of FDR's famed "brain trust", helping to set the policies of that administration for his environmental work, while he was writing 33 books and working with several government agencies.

## Rowland H. Macy *1822-1919*

The founder of the famous R.H. Macy department store, now a large chain, got his start in the retail dry goods business in a store on Merrimack Street in Haverhill.

It was there that he pioneered many of the techniques that changed the way large department stores did business. He started underselling his competitors; selling for cash only, at a small profit, and using new marketing and advertising methods.

His Thanksgiving Parade, now a national holiday attraction, had a modest start in Haverhill.

His store failed in Haverhill, but his experience here, plus generous financing from Caleb Dustin Hunking of this city, helped him to build the business that made him nationally prominent.

## Ann Haseltine Judson *1789-1826*

This Bradford native was the first woman to leave America as a Christian missionary to "heathen" when she accompanied her husband to Burma in 1812.

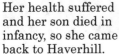
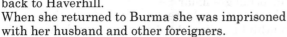

Her health suffered and her son died in infancy, so she came back to Haverhill. When she returned to Burma she was imprisoned with her husband and other foreigners.

After her release she started a new mission at Amherst in Burma, where she died in 1826. She wrote about her adventures. "Account of the American Baptist Mission to the Burman Empire."

A monument on the Bradford Common is a tribute to that missionary work.

## Frank Fontaine *1920-1978*

"Frankie" Fontaine began his comedy career in the night clubs and taverns of Haverhill, starting in the Lafayette Square area.

His ability took him to a growing world of entertainment that moved through the various venues. From the clubs he went to theaters, to radio, to television and to the movies.

It was in television that he gained national recognition for his talent. He had created several characters, but it was one, Crazy Guggenheim, that enabled him to form a team with top star Jackie Gleason that reached into millions of American homes.

From the little bars of Haverhill to the biggest bar on television, Frankie Fontaine kept them laughing for years.

## Daniel Appleton *1785-1849*

Mr. Appleton started his business career in 1813 when he opened a dry goods store on Water Street.

He moved the business to Boston in 1817, and then moved again, this time to New York City, in 1825, where he started the House of Appleton.

In 1831, he began publishing books as D. Appleton and Co., and became the major America publisher of European authors, many of them controversial, like Darwin, Huxley, and Spencer. He published works of Catholic and Jewish writers.

He was among the first to print books in Spanish for South Americans, and was one of the first to print children's books.

## Winfield Townley Scott *1910-1968*

This 1927 graduate of Haverhill High School became a poet and author of many distinguished literary works, principally poetry which brought him many scholastic and journalistic honors.

One of his poems honored another member of the Hall of Fame, another Haverhill poet, under the title, "Mr. Whittier and Other Poems."

Mr. Scott became literary editor of the Providence Journal and a trustee of the Providence Public Library with several awards, including Phi Beta Kappa poet at Brown, Tufts, and Harvard.

He was named literary editor of the New Mexican in the 1960s and was editor of three books before his death in Santa Fe in 1968.

## Nathaniel Saltonstall *1639-1707*

The original home, on the site of the buttonwoods, home of the Haverhill historical society, was built by Mr. Saltonstall.

He married Elizabeth Ward, daughter of Haverhill's first minister, John Ward, whose reputed home is on the grounds of the buttonwoods.

His political career included being a representative; town clerk, 1679-86; colonel of the Essex regiment; assistant to the governor's council and later a member of the council.

He was appointed a judge of the court of Oyer and Terminez in 1692 and had the distinction of refusing to serve at the infamous Salem witch trials that year.

## Benjamin Greenleaf *1786-1864*

His career as a teacher in Haverhill was what led to his writing a series of books about mathematics that sold more than a million copies between 1835 and 1864.

After graduating from North Dartmouth, he became principal of the Haverhill grammar school. In 1813, he began a career with the youthful Bradford Academy that later lasted until 1836.

He was elected to the state legislature in 1837, and later spent years making calculations for almanacs and advancing public education.

The Greenleaf School is named for him and a Bradford street bears the family name.

## James R. Nichols *1819-1888*

Mr. Nichols' lasting legacy to Haverhill is Winnekenni castle, which he had built in 1874 as a summer home and as a site for chemical and agricultural experiments.

He opened a drug store in Haverhill in 1843 and founded a wholesale drug chemical business in Boston.

His inventions included a soda water dispenser, a fire extinguisher and an improved hot-air furnace. He was also the founder of the first publication devoted to chemistry in a popular sense.

He was president of the Vermont and Canadian Railroad and a director of the Boston and Maine Railroad: he founded the Haverhill Monday Evening Club and the Whittier Club.

## Enoch Bartlett *1779-1860*

The name of Mr. Bartlett is prominent today in every fruit display in marks throughout this country, and in other lands as well.

He was the developer of the famous Bartlett pear, a variety he developed the first displayed before the Massachusetts horticultural society, an organization he helped to found and which he served as vice president in 1829-37.

He was in dry goods business in Boston and chanced to be in England at the start of the war of 1812, He brought back with him the last

shipload of English goods to reach Boston and he realized a "sizable amount of profit." With that, he bought a mansion in Roxbury and cultivated his interest in horticulture, leading to the development of the Bartlett pear.

## Muriel Sanders Draper *1886-1952*

Born in Haverhill to the telephone-rich Sanders family, Muriel moved from Haverhill schools to social circles where she met and married tenor and concert singer Paul Draper.

That took her to a life in Europe where she became a celebrated hostess, entertaining many famous people of the era before World War I in France and Italy.

She returned to the U.S. but became interested in Russia, visited Moscow and, during World War II, promoted friendship with our wartime allies.

She later founded and directed women's federations, here and abroad, and spoke at times about oppression of labor and minorities in the U.S.

## Louis Alter *1902-1980*

A musical career that started at age 13 playing piano in Haverhill theaters took Louis Alter to a place in the "Songwriters Hall of Fame" and many other honors as a composer of popular music.

His songs included Manhattan Serenade; You Turned the Tables on Me; Rainbow on the River and the music for the first outdoor color movie.

He accompanied many of the outstanding singers of the stage and movies and composed music for many revues and pictures. He was a piano soloist for concerts including some in the Hollywood Bowl. As a member of the Army Air Corps in World War II he entertained fellow soldiers.

At Haverhill High School his band played for dances; his later music took him to the top ranks of his profession.

He is buried at Children of Israel Cemetery in Haverhill.

## Donald J. Atwood *1924-1993*

From Haverhill High School, his career took him to Massachusetts Institute of Technology and then to General Motors.

At GM, his business and administrative skills took him to the presidency of two divisions of the huge company. He was Chairman of the Board when he was called by President George H.W. Bush to become Deputy Secretary of Defense.

When the Gulf War started, Mr. Atwood and General Colin Powell worked together in the Pentagon to rally and direct the American military forces that took part.

He was the deputy to Richard Cheney, later to become the Vice-President of the United States under President George W Bush, son of Mr. Atwood's Commander-in-Chief.

## Gladys Emerson Cook *1895-1975*

One of the world's foremost painters of animal portraits, Miss Cook was also an author. She was famed for her Christmas cards and circus posters as well as her prized drawings of cats and dogs.

Her work is in the Library of Congress, the Metropolitan Museum and the Smithsonian Institution.

She was listed in "Who's Who in America," "Who's Who in Art" and other prestigious groupings.

She was a fellow of the Royal Society of Arts of England and a member of the American Society of Illustrators.

## Gert Swazey *1855-1934*

Gert Swazey's circus career made her one of Haverhill's most colorful products.

With Barnum and Bailey's and other circuses, she perfected a four-horse bareback riding act that included a leap through a ring of fire.

She was believed to be the first female circus performer to wear tights.

From a tempestuous childhood that included exclusion from Bradford Academy, she toured the country as a performer, then returned to Haverhill to live out her last years in poverty.

## Joseph C. Goyette *1884-1969*

Mr. Goyette went to work in the shoe factories of Haverhill at age 14 and in 1941 he helped to organize the United Shoe Workers Union in the city, becoming manager-treasurer in 1942. He later was an organizer for the union.

In the 1950s, he became a Marshall Plan worker with the State Department. In that capacity he traveled more than 100,000 miles in France, Germany, Norway, Denmark, Italy, Mexico, Guatemala and Panama.

In those countries, he helped with production and labor-management relations in the shoe industry.

## Dudley Eaton Fitts *1903-1968*

After his graduation from Haverhill High School (1921) and Harvard, Mr. Fitts began a teaching and writing career that earned him distinction as a poet and translator.

He taught at Choate School and Phillips Andover, and his first book of poetry was published in 1931.

In the years following, his poetry appeared in many magazines. He was awarded the Golden Rose of the New England Poetry Society.

He was elected a fellow of the National Institute of Arts and Letters. In addition, he was recognized and appreciated for his translations of Greek and Latin literature.

## Cora Chase *1892-1984*

Cora Chase Williamson was the outstanding musical performer to come out of Haverhill.

As a girl in the city's public schools, she displayed a voice that was clearly of classical quality.

Her musical studies took her to Italy, where she made her debut as a coloratura soprano.

She joined the Metropolitan Opera Company in New York in 1920 and signed a recording contract with RCA Victor, after being named "America's Greatest Coloratura."

Cora Chase retired from singing after her marriage to a man she met as a child at the Burnham School, New York Times writer Samuel T. Williamson.

## John A. Bellairs *1938-1991*

Mr. Bellairs was a best-selling author, known nationally for his series of scary thriller books for children.

He also wrote adult novels, but said he was most comfortable writing for children because, it was said, his imagination was stuck at age 10.

He not only enjoyed writing for children, but was also happy reading to them and talking to them. He was a frequent visitor at the Haverhill Public Library and in the schools in the area.

Mr. Bellairs said he hoped he was encouraging children to not only read but also to write themselves.

He was a native of Michigan, but made Haverhill his home after he started teaching at Merrimack College.

## Andre Dubus *1937-1999*

Before he died unexpectedly in 1999, Andre Dubus had earned a strong national reputation, especially among writers, for the excellence of his literary work.

In his prime specialty, short stories, he often included the atmosphere and the people he lived among in Haverhill.

He received numerous awards, including a Guggenheim Fellowship and a MacArthur "genius grant." He was a finalist for a Pulitzer Prize and the National Book Critics Circle award. He was a Bradford College professor and an inspiration to his friends and to his family. In return for rewards, he held free writing clinics.

Many of the country's best authors helped him when he was seriously injured in an automobile accident, showing their respect for him and his work.

## A. Raymond Tye *1923-2010*

Tye was the son of Kosovo immigrants. He graduated from Haverhill High School, studied at Tufts College and planned to become a social worker. He was wounded during World War II when he served in the Army as an adjutant to General George Patton. After the war, he worked for United Liquors in Boston and worked his way up from warehouse worker to president.

As a philanthropist, Tye quietly paid medical costs of those unable to afford life-saving treatment. He was the face of the Ray Tye Medical Aid Foundation, created by his wife and friends, which continues to provide live-saving medical treatment to those who can't afford it.

Tye also helped the Boston Celtics. During the organization's early years he helped Red Auerbach meet the payroll.

## Ezekial J.M. Hale *1813-1881*

Hale, a Haverhill native who became a business tycoon, also became president of the Manchester & Lawrence Railroad.

After Haverhill was incorporated as a city in 1870, Hale donated land and pledged one half of the funds to build the city's first public library if its citizens raised the other half. To assure the library's continued success, he left $100,000 in a trust to pay for maintenance and for the perpetual addition to its collection of books.

He also gave $50,000 and an estate on Kent Street to be used for a hospital. Hale also commissioned the bronze statue of Hanna Dustin in 1879. That statue is the only statue of a woman in Haverhill and is believed to be the first statue of a woman in the United States.

## POETRY

# A Day

Talk not of sad November, when a day
Of warm, glad sunshine fills the sky of noon,
And a wind, borrowed from some morn of June,
Stirs the brown grasses and the leafless spray.

On the unfrosted pool the pillared pines
Lay their long shafts of shadow: the small rill,
Singing a pleasant song of summer still,
A line of silver, down the hill-slope shines.

Hushed the bird-voices and the hum of bees,
In the thin grass the crickets pipe no more;
But still the squirrel hoards his winter store,
And drops his nut-shells from the shag-bark trees.

Softly the dark green hemlocks whisper: high
Above, the spires of yellowing larches show,
Where the woodpecker and home-loving crow
And jay and nut-hatch winter's threat defy.

O gracious beauty, ever new and old!
O sights and sounds of nature, doubly dear
When the low sunshine warns the closing year
Of snow-blown fields and waves of Arctic cold!

Close to my heart I fold each lovely thing
The sweet day yields; and, not disconsolate,
With the calm patience of the woods I wait
For leaf and blossom when God gives us Spring!

*- John Greenleaf Whittier*

54

## Kenoza Lake

As Adam did in Paradise,
To-day the primal right we claim
Fair mirror of the woods and skies,
We give to thee a name.

Lake of the pickerel!--let no more
The echoes answer back, 'Great Pond,'
But sweet Kenoza, from thy shore
And watching hills beyond,

Let Indian ghosts, if such there be
Who ply unseen their shadowy lines,
Call back the ancient name to thee,
As with the voice of pines.

The shores we trod as barefoot boys,
The nutted woods we wandered through,
To friendship, love, and social joys
We consecrate anew.

Here shall the tender song be sung,
And memory's dirges soft and low,
And wit shall sparkle on the tongue,
And mirth shall overflow,

Harmless as summer lightning plays
From a low, hidden cloud by night,
A light to set the hills ablaze,
But not a bolt to smite.

In sunny South and prairied West
Are exiled hearts remembering still,
As bees their hive, as birds their nest,
The homes of Haverhill.

They join us in our rites to-day;
And, listening, we may hear, erelong,
From inland lake and ocean bay,
The echoes of our song.

Kenoza! o'er no sweeter lake
Shall morning break or noon-cloud sail,--
No fairer face than thine shall take
The sunset's golden veil.

Long be it ere the tide of trade
Shall break with harsh-resounding din
The quiet of thy banks of shade,
And hills that fold thee in.

Still let thy woodlands hide the hare,
The shy loon sound his trumpet-note,
Wing-weary from his fields of air,
The wild-goose on thee float.

Thy peace rebuke our feverish stir,
Thy beauty our deforming strife;
Thy woods and waters minister
The healing of their life.

And sinless Mirth, from care released,
Behold, unawed, thy mirrored sky,
Smiling as smiled on Cana's feast
The Master's loving eye.

And when the summer day grows dim,
And light mists walk thy mimic sea,
Revive in us the thought of Him
Who walked on Galilee!

- *John Greenleaf Whittier*

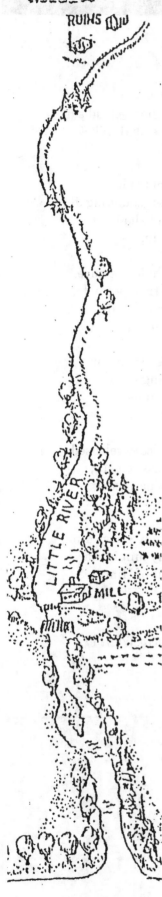

## Haverhill History Resources

Chase, George Wingate, *The History* of *Haverhill, Massachusetts*.
Camden, ME: Picton Press, 1997.

Cogswell, Hon. John B. D., *Haverhill, 1640-1888*.
Philadelphia, PA: J. W. Lewis & Co., 1888.

Freeman, Donald C., *The Story* of *Winnekenni, 1640-1976*. Haverhill, MA:
The Board of Directors of the Winnekenni Foundation, 1977.

Freeman, Donald C., John B. Pickard and Roland H. Woodwell,
*Whittier and Whittierland*. Haverhill, MA: HPL Press, 1976.

Frothingham, E. G., *A Ramble About Haverhill in My Boyhood Days*.
A paper read before the Haverhill Historical Society, 1921.

Gage, Mary Elaine and James E. Gage, Stories *Carved in* Stone.
Amesbury, MA: Powwow River Books, 2003.

Garwich, Pat, *Haverhill Trivia*. Haverhill, MA, 1989

Kingsbury, J. D., Memorial *History* of *Bradford, Mass*. Haverhill, MA:
C. C. Morse & Son, 1882.

Obert, Christopher, P. and Nancy S. Obert, *Legendary Locals*,
Charleston, SC, Arcadia Publishing, 2011.

O'Malley, Patricia Trainor, *Images ofAmerica, Bradford, the End of an Era*.
Dover, NH: Arcadia Publishing, 1996.

O'Malley, Patricia Trainor, *Images of America, Haverhill,
Massachusetts From* Town to City. Dover, NH: Arcadia Publishing, 1997.

O'Malley, Patricia Trainor, *Images of America, Italians in Haverhill*.
Charleston, SC: Arcadia Publishing, 2001.

O'Malley, Patricia Trainor, *Images of America, The Irish in Haverhill*.
Dover, NH: Arcadia Publishing, 1998.

O'Malley, Patricia Trainor, *Images of America, The Irish in Haverhill
Volume 11*. Charleston, SC: Arcadia Publishing, 1999.

O'Malley, Patricia Trainor and Paul H. Tedesco, *A New England* City:
*Haverhill, Massachusetts*. Northridge, CA: Windsor Publications, Inc., 1987.

Pupils of the eighth grade, *A City Grows, The Story of Haverhill, Mass*.
Haverhill, MA: The Printing Department of the Charles W. Arnold Trade
School, 1949.

Tedesco, Paul H., *Haverhill* Celebrates *Haverhill's 350', 1640-1990*.
Haverhill, MA: HPL Press, 1990.

Thayer, Maud Palmer, *The Beginnings* of *Bradford*. Haverhill, MA:
Record Publishing Company, 1928.

Turner, Charles W., *Remembering Haverhill, Stories from the Merrimack
Valley*. Charleston, SC: The History Press, 2008.

# Haverhill, Massachusetts TRIVIA BOOK

Revision 3, April 2013

This project is supported in part by a grant from the Haverhill Cultural Council, a local agency which is supported by the Massachusetts Cultural Council, a state agency.

## Acknowledgment:

Revisions to the Haverhill Trivia Book were made with the assistance of students in the Haverhill High School *History of Haverhill* Course.

**History of Haverhill Class First Semester 2012- 2013**

*From left to right: Chris Heywood, Michael Moriarty, Selena Rosario, Dylan Copeland, Kathleen O'Neil, Jeremy Blaisdell, Stephen Alongi, Dan Young, Josseline Medrano, Angelica Rosario, Chris DiChristofaro, Patrick Rich, Anthony Cresta, Javier Colon Santiago, Jennifer Mendez-Medina, Mr. Brown*

*Not in photo: Miranda Clough, Max Read, Rochelle Rothermel, Michael Swenson*

## Special Thanks Trivia:

Q: In 2012, who did E. Philip Brown enlist to help with all of his documents and pictures to create this trivia book?

A: A designer named Paul M. Favreau, a resident of Haverhill who lives in the area known as Walnut Square.

## About the authors:

Phil Brown, currently a history teacher at Haverhill High School, has a bachelor's degree in Political Science from the University of Massachusetts/Amherst. He also holds a masters degree in Applied Management from Lesley University. Phil is also a Certified Advanced Facilitator for the University of Phoenix. He and his wife, Chrisi, have two children and live in Haverhill, Massachusetts

Pat Garwich is a retired sixth grade teacher from Consentino School in Haverhill, MA. She holds a bachelors degree from Lowell State College and a masters degree from Lowell University. Pat moved to Haverhill with her family in 1960. She has always been fascinated by the history of the city in which she chose to live and work.

Printed in the United States
by Baker & Taylor Publisher Services

Printed in the United States
by Baker & Taylor Publisher Services